Loren Dean, Matt McGrath and John Spencer in a scene from the New York production of "Amulets Against The Dragon Forces." Setting designed by David Potts.

AMULETS AGAINST THE DRAGON FORCES

BY PAUL ZINDEL

DRAMATISTS
PLAY SERVICE
INC.

SOUND EFFECTS
The following is a list of sound effects referenced in this play:
Auto sounds
Glass breaking
Telephone ring

AMULETS AGAINST THE DRAGON FORCES was presented by Circle Repertory Company (Tanya Berezin, Artistic Director) on April 6, 1989.

It was directed by B. Rodney Marriott; the set was by David Potts; the costumes were by Walker Hicklin; the lights were by Dennis Parichy; and the sound was by Chuck London Media/Stewart Werner, with original music by Norman L. Berman. The production stage manager was M.A. Howard and the fight director was Rick Sordelet. The cast was as follows:

CHRIS	Matt McGrath
HAROLD	Loren Dean
FLOYD	John Spencer
MRS. BOYD	Deborah Hedwall
MRS. DIPARDI	Ruby Holbrook
ATTENDANT #1	Jerome Preston Bates
ATTENDANT #2	John Viscardi
JOEY	John Viscardi
RICHIE	Robert Gladding
ROOCHIE	James Gregory Smith
LEROY	Jerome Preston Bates
ROSEMARY	Carrena Lukas

CHARACTERS

FLOYD DIPARDI — a shipyard worker
MRS. BOYD — a practical nurse
CHRIS — her son
HAROLD — Floyd's friend; a street kid
MRS. DIPARDI — Floyd's dying mother

TWO AMBULANCE ATTENDANTS (can double for "party boys")

THE SETTING

Like destiny itself, the set is fragmented, in motion, secretly inevitable. We suspect a bungalow made of wood, touched by shutters and beams. As the realities clarify, we will have seen areas in which our story was lived and told: there is a jalousie porch with a screen door; a kitchen area, old and abused, with — of all things — *a crystal chandelier* hanging over the kitchen table; a living room with overstuffed squatting pieces dominated by a tallboy used to hoard liquor; and a wall of shelves spilling with books. The master bedroom has a queen-sized, vulgar bed, with a dyed sheepskin cover — and a smaller rear bedroom hides like the past down a dark hallway. A "bumper" pool table squats somewhere; and above all is the attic loft, a slanting roof with a bed for a boy, a sanctuary from whose shadows life itself could begin anew.

ACT I

Scene 1: Morning
Scene 2: Later that afternoon
Scene 3: Later that night
Scene 4: Evening, the next week
Scene 5: Later that evening

ACT II

Scene 1: Morning, the next day
Scene 2: Evening

Staten Island 1955

AMULETS AGAINST THE DRAGON FORCES

ACT ONE

SCENE ONE

A spot slowly comes up on Chris. He stands Downstage wearing an overcoat which is much too large for him. He holds forth a small handmade figure representing himself.

CHRIS. (*Fearfully.*)
Appear . . . appear, if you must . . .
What shape will you be?
What name will you have?
A monster from the darkest night?
A serpent with a thousand heads?

Where must I go?
Who will you be?

God . . .
Beast . . .
What mystery? . . .
MRS. BOYD'S VOICE. Chris! Hurry up, Chris . . . we're leaving . . . (*Chris runs off into darkness as there is the scream of an ambulance. The lights come up on the set. Harold, a young kid, athletic, runs in from the front door and to Floyd's bedroom.*)
HAROLD. They're here! They're here! Hey, get up! Come on, Floyd, get up!

7

FLOYD'S VOICE. Don't worry about it. (*Harold runs back to the kitchen to look out the door.*)

HAROLD. They're taking her out! They're all out there, everybody's out there! (*Floyd enters, putting on his robe. He is a muscular worker whose body is only slightly drifting toward the distortions of chronic drinking and neglect.*)

FLOYD. Did you make my coffee?

HAROLD. Mrs. Larson's hanging right out her window.

FLOYD. My robe's wet.

HAROLD. Floyd, hurry up! Hurry up!

FLOYD. I don't like you using my robe! (*Floyd sits in the chair.*)

HAROLD. Here comes the stretcher. They're rolling her up the driveway. Do you want me to get out? I think I should get out.

FLOYD. You just stay and pour me a cup of coffee. (*Mrs. Boyd, dressed in a nurse's white uniform, leads a procession of two Ambulance Attendants carrying Mrs. Dipardi on a gurney. Chris, Mrs. Boyd's son, wearing a very large overcoat, trails along behind them, lugging two suitcases and a few shopping bags. Mrs. Boyd is around forty, and her hair frames deep-set, darting eyes in a way that hints of a mixture of great vulnerability and lurking hysteria. Mrs. Dipardi, we will discover, is Floyd's mother. She is pale and gaunt.*)

MRS. BOYD. (*Directing the maneuver as they enter.*) Please be careful! Watch what you're doing!

ATTENDANT #1. We *are*, lady.

MRS. BOYD. I told you to be careful. She is in great pain. Just think of yourself in her position. Watch out for the door.

ATTENDANT #2. Don't worry about it.

MRS. BOYD. Think of her as your own mother. (*Harold rushes to help hold ajar the screen door while the others struggle through. Mrs. Boyd holds back as the two Attendants carry Mrs. DiPardi into the house. Chris stays out on the porch.*)

ATTENDANT #1. Get out of the way. Out of the way. (*Harold takes a wet cloth from the sink to Floyd.*)

MRS. BOYD. I asked you to be gentle. Please be gentle with her.

ATTENDANT #2. You make it sound like we're dribbling her.

8

MRS. BOYD. I didn't ask for any of your unkind comments. Please watch it, or she's going to roll off.

ATTENDANT #2. She's not rolling anywhere.

MRS. BOYD. I'll report you if that's what I have to do. She's a human being and she deserves respect.

ATTENDANT #1. Don't we all!

MRS. BOYD. Are you all right, Mrs. DiPardi?

FLOYD. How many stingers did I have last night?

HAROLD. Eight.

FLOYD. It feels like somebody's got a jackhammer on my skull. (*Mrs. DiPardi begins to make moaning sounds. Mrs. Boyd enters into the kitchen behind the procession, carrying a medical bag, Mrs. DiPardi's small suitcase and a clipboard. After wheeling Mrs. DiPardi D.C., Attendant #2 exits back out the door.*)

MRS. BOYD. I'm Nurse Boyd. Are you Mr. Floyd DiPardi? (*She deposits her wares on the table.*)

FLOYD. (*Rising and crossing to the table.*) Well, it's a good thing you came to the right house, I'd say.

MRS. BOYD. The registry told me you had to work at the shipyard today, that you couldn't come to the hospital.

FLOYD. Yeah, but I decided to take the morning off. (*Mrs. DiPardi moans.*) Hi, Mom, how you doing, old girl? Huh? How you doing? It's good to have you home. Welcome home, Mom. (*He can barely look at her. Mrs. DiPardi moans again.*)

HAROLD. Should I baste the roast now, Floyd? I think it's time to baste the roast.

FLOYD. There, you see, we made you an eye of the round, Mom. We made you an eye of the round.

MRS. BOYD. She's on a special diet, more gentle foods. I'll be doing the cooking for her. (*Attendant #2 returns with the "intravenous".*)

FLOYD. Oh, you know, that's a real disappointment, isn't it! We make your favorite food and she comes in here and says you aren't going to be having any.

ATTENDANT #1. Could you discuss the menu later?

ATTENDANT #2. Where do you want us to put her?

MRS. DIPARDI. (*Rather faintly; with great effort.*) Please . . . something to drink . . . please . . .

MRS. BOYD. She's dehydrating. She needs fluids. Where's

9

her room? (*Mrs. Boyd gets a glass of water from Harold at the sink.*)

FLOYD. Right down the end of the hall. The suite on the right. (*The Attendants start pushing the gurney toward hallway. Mrs. Boyd's voice stops them.*)

MRS. BOYD. Wait a minute. She's got to have clean linens, proper "ventilation." I didn't know this was going to be a bungalow. If you haven't rented the correct equipment, she's not going to be staying here. (*After Mrs. Boyd gives Mrs. DiPardi a drink, she hands the glass to Floyd and exits to check the room down the hall. Mrs. DiPardi holds out for more water, so he gives the glass to Harold, but Mrs. DiPardi won't accept it from Harold.*)

FLOYD. (*To Attendants.*) Hey, you guys want a hit of Old Turkey?

ATTENDANT #1. Well, we're not allowed to drink on the job.

FLOYD. Who you kiddin'? Harold, give the guys a "couple of fingers." You guys do anything you want nowadays. Come on, have a belt.

ATTENDANT #2. Hey, you know we did everything we could.

ATTENDANT #1. Yeah, we gave your mom special service. We took her down from the sixth floor at Ewing.

ATTENDANT #2. We had to go down the Memorial elevator and then push her up on a ramp . . .

FLOYD. Oh God, yes, that's a lot of work, those ramps.

ATTENDANT #1. Oh yeah. (*They toast as Mrs. Boyd appears back from the hallway.*)

MRS. BOYD. Well, I'm glad you rented the oxygen and the air mattress. She's got terrible lesions from all the neglect at the hospital.

FLOYD. Well, then, you're going to get rid of them, aren't you? Get that isopropyl and those fingertips going.

MRS. BOYD. There are some pains I can't soothe. Only those who love her can do that. (*To the Attendants.*) You boys stop drinking or I'll let Delancy know and you'll be discharged. You know that as well as I do.

FLOYD. Oh, leave the boys alone. (*Floyd walks to the front door, looks out.*)

ATTENDANT #2. Look, we trotted the intravenous, the glucose. You had us running like dogs.

MRS. BOYD. You did what you get paid to do. Go hook everything up. I mean *now*, and I'm not kidding. (*The Attendants leave Mrs. DiPardi on the gurney and exit down the hall with the medical equipment and supplies. Mrs. Boyd focuses on Harold.*) Who is this?

FLOYD. Who is it? Well, it's Harold Farley, Mr. Harold Farley. Jesus, Mary and Joseph, I didn't even introduce you, did I? Harold, this is Practical Nurse Boyd. (*Then he turns his attention to Chris — whom he has noticed is still out on the porch. Harold, embarrassed, exits into Floyd's bedroom.*) And who is that?

MRS. BOYD. The registry told you I was bringing my son. (*Ordering.*) Chris! Get in here!

CHRIS. Okay, just a minute . . .

FLOYD. Oh, yeah, that's a son, isn't it?

MRS. BOYD. They didn't say anything about *you* having a boy at the house.

FLOYD. Well, there *is* one . . .

MRS. BOYD. I told you to get in here! (*Chris enters with suitcases and shopping bags. Mrs. DiPardi begins to make loud moaning sounds again and bang the gurney's aluminum retainers, trying to explain something. Her eyes seem fixed on one spot.*)

FLOYD. (*Forcing himself.*) Hey, mom, what's the matter? Can I get you something? You want to see the eye of the round, that what you want?

MRS. DIPARDI. No . . . oh . . . oh . . .

MRS. BOYD. (*Fussing.*) You just relax and let me take care of everything. (*To Floyd, very loudly, manipulatively, while he crosses around the table.*) She's a lovely lady. It won't be long before she'll be up on her feet going around like the old days.

FLOYD. Yeah, she'll be going around . . .

MRS. BOYD. (*To Mrs. DiPardi.*) You'll be running around taking care of everybody just like you always did.

FLOYD. Oh, yeah — mom was always a great little homemaker.

MRS. BOYD. (*Continuing to Mrs. DiPardi.*) And while you're

11

laid up, we're going to take care of you for awhile. I'm sure your son is very happy to do a little for *you* now.

MRS. DIPARDI. (*Trying to say something.*) Uh . . . uh . . . did . . . uh . . .

MRS. BOYD. What? The chandelier? Oh, my, I've never seen a chandelier in a kitchen before.

FLOYD. I believe it.

MRS. BOYD. Is that your chandelier, Mrs. DiPardi? That's your chandelier, isn't it? It's a delicate and lovely accent.

FLOYD. Very French.

MRS. BOYD. You gave this bungalow a woman's touch, didn't you, Mrs. DiPardi?

MRS. DIPARDI. Uh . . . uh . . .

MRS. BOYD. You really love delicate things, don't you?

FLOYD. She's not staring at the chandelier. She's looking at the button open on top of your uniform.

MRS. BOYD. (*Embarrassed.*) Oh, I'm sorry. I lost the button, and I didn't have a safety pin. I didn't even know it was open.

MRS. DIPARDI. (*Motioning to Floyd with an anger only the dying know.*) Did you get a good look at her tits? Did you get a good look at her tits?

MRS. BOYD. (*Shocked.*) Now you don't mean to be saying that. That's all the drugs. The poisons in those experimental drugs.

FLOYD. Naw. That's how she always talks.

MRS. BOYD. You're a lovely lady, a lovely lady . . . (*The Attendants return.*)

MRS. BOYD. Would you please get her down the hall now? (*The Attendants begin to take Mrs. DiPardi down the hall, led by Mrs. Boyd.*)

ATTENDANT #2. Sure, we'll get her down.

MRS. BOYD. And you be gentle with her.

ATTENDANT #1. Yeah, we'll be gentle as lambs.

MRS. BOYD. She's a wonderful woman. A delicate woman.

ATTENDANT #2. Like a porcelain doll. We've got a porcelain doll here.

MRS. BOYD. Watch out you don't hit anything.

ATTENDANT #1. We're not going to sock her head against the wall.

MRS. BOYD. Just watch out. (*They exit into the bedroom, leaving Chris and Floyd alone. Floyd gets another drink.*)

CHRIS. I really like your house, Mr. DiPardi. My father used to drive me out here to Prince's Bay, and we'd watch a big turtle some man had as a pet with a chain through its shell. Dad lives in St. Augustine, Florida now, near the Ripley's Believe It or Not Museum — which he says has a real shrunken head and the lifetime nail clippings of a Benedictine monk. He and my mother got a divorce when I was three.

FLOYD. He lasted that long with her, huh?

CHRIS. He's a Florida state trooper now, but he was a New York City policeman — 123rd Precinct — before that, and every Thanksgiving he'd give us a free turkey and on Fourth of Julys, he'd confiscate cherry bombs for me. I really like your decor, Mr. DiPardi.

MRS. BOYD. (*Reentering.*) Where will my son sleep?

FLOYD. (*Pointing in the direction of the attic room.*) Oh, up there. Up, *up* there.

CHRIS. Where?

FLOYD. Some people might call it a crawl space, but it's really an attic with very exciting "*decor.*"

MRS. BOYD. (*To Chris.*) If it's unsuitable, you won't be staying in it.

FLOYD. Unsuitable? It's a regular penthouse.

MRS. BOYD. It's up those stairs?

FLOYD. Oh, yeah. Let me show you "Treetops."

MRS. BOYD. (*To Chris.*) I'll be right down. Just don't worry. If it's not decent, we'll find something that is.

CHRIS. It'll be fine, mom. It's just like Mrs. Thomas' Greenwood Lake house when we visited her and she cooked that whole pound of bacon in a single frying pan. (*Mrs. Boyd and Floyd start upstairs. Harold returns and Chris takes a good look at him as he fusses with the roast in the kitchen.*) Hi. I'm Chris. Are you related to him? His nephew or something?

HAROLD. No, I'm no relation.

CHRIS. I just thought you might be. It's really a very nice kitchen. Good lighting really is important in a kitchen.

HAROLD. The chandelier's on a "re-estat." Did you ever

13

see a "re-estat?" (*Turning on the switch.*) You turn this, and the light goes up and down. You can make it very bright or as low as candles. Floyd made it, the "re-estat."

CHRIS. I admire people with the spirit to be original like that, in all aspects of their lives. I read about a man in Houston which has no zoning laws. He kept a gorilla in his kitchen which ate shell steaks. (*Floyd and Mrs. Boyd arrive up at the threshold to the attic room. Mrs. Boyd goes in, but Floyd avoids setting even a foot inside.*)

FLOYD. I know it must be quite a comedown from the Staten Island Excelsior. That was where you were staying, wasn't it? The Staten Island Excelsior? Or was it the Ritz Hotel of St. George? (*Mrs. Boyd starts down the stairs, with Floyd behind her.*)

MRS. BOYD. (*To Chris.*) It's not too bad.

FLOYD. Nothing's perfect, of course. No closet space, moths the size of your fist, and you have to walk around like a hunchback, but it's cozy.

MRS. BOYD. (*To Chris.*) Take your things up. I've got to check on the attendants. (*Mrs. Boyd and Floyd exit down the hall, Mrs. Boyd into Mrs. DiPardi's room and Floyd into his own bedroom.*)

HAROLD. Floyd bought me a new tooth.

CHRIS. A tooth?

HAROLD. I lost one near the front, and it showed if I smiled. I had nits, too.

CHRIS. A missing tooth and nits at the same time?

HAROLD. That was before I met Floyd. I don't have nits now.

CHRIS. When I was in P.S. 8, nits swept through the whole fourth grade, and kids put kerosene on their heads and wore stocking caps to get rid of them. I heard Woolworth's Five and Ten Cent Store made a fortune selling fine-toothed combs.

HAROLD. I also had poor hair follicles. Actually, I was a physical wreck before I met Floyd.

CHRIS. Where did you meet Floyd?

HAROLD. He was going by in a car, and he stopped.

CHRIS. (*Crossing to front door.*) Is that his car in the

14

driveway—the two-tone Chevy? It looks like it's in really good shape.

HAROLD. Yeah. That's a '54, but he's already ordered a brand new 1955, two-tone red. I had malnutrition, you know. He's been teaching me how to eat right.

CHRIS. (*Returning to the table.*) That's really good. In general science class, they had pictures of mice when they didn't drink their orange juice and they used to waltz in circles! Where does he work?

HAROLD. At Staten Island Shipyard. He usually works the night shift watching the compressor. Floyd's my best friend.

CHRIS. He just stopped for you in his car?

HAROLD. Listen, I have to get parsley. Floyd likes it if I put parsley around the roast, you know, and you eat a little afterwards and it takes away the taste. Tell him I went to get it, okay?

CHRIS. I don't know much about herbs and garnishings, but I understand they're very crucial in exotic cooking.

HAROLD. Just say I went down to the A&P, okay? He's been yelling at me a lot lately. Do you want to go to a movie some night? Maybe you and I could get out to a movie? A new one opens at the Victory.

CHRIS. Okay. I like movies. I haven't been to the Victory since they had that live roller skater at the matinee, and you could line up to be swung around on the stage. I got swung around a lot of times. (*Harold exits. Chris opens the refrigerator. He takes a bottle of milk and drinks as Floyd comes back from the hallway.*)

FLOYD. In this house we use a glass, young fella.

CHRIS. Oh, I'm sorry. I know most people keep their glasses right above the sink, but one patient we had, her daughter used to keep them locked up because they were Baccarat. (*The Attendants come up the hall, start out door with the gurney. Chris picks up the suitcases and shopping bags, leaving his mother's suitcase by the pool table.*)

ATTENDANT #2. (*To Floyd.*) We're not supposed to set things up like that. I don't care what she tells you. We're supposed to handle only the gurney . . .

ATTENDANT #1. We gave your mother first-rate care,

Mr. DiPardi. She's a great lady.

ATTENDANT #2. A terrific personality. We really went out of our way.

FLOYD. Oh, and I really appreciate it, you know. You guys are a couple of angels, you really are. I know you wouldn't dream of taking a gratuity, but maybe you could make an exception — force yourselves. Just a few bucks. Here.

ATTENDANT #1. Well, I can see you're a gentleman and a scholar. You'd be surprised, we get stifled a lot.

FLOYD. Yeah. Well, you just never know where you're going to get a good tip from these days, do you?

ATTENDANT #2. You can say that again, and good luck to you.

ATTENDANT #1. It's been a pleasure. A real pleasure. And miracles can happen. We'll say a prayer.

FLOYD. Ah, you're the salt of the earth, boys . . . the salt of the earth. (*They exit. Floyd has followed them to the door.*)

CHRIS. I think I'd better get my stuff upstairs. I brought my own hangers . . .

FLOYD. (*Zeroing in.*) Say, kid — I *know* you, don't I? Don't I know you?

CHRIS. No, I don't think so. (*Chris puts his bags down and crosses to pool table.*) It really amazes me how many people on earth look just like other people. One woman who lived in our hotel had a deep voice and a little brow, she was a pastry chef, and twice a year she had friends who were in an all-girl band at the Top Hat Club and they used to play "Honeysuckle Rose" whenever she walked in the door. And the incredible thing was that all the girls in the band had deep voices and little brows just like the pastry chef. Charles Darwin should have really studied them like he did finches in the Galapagos Islands.

FLOYD. You ever go to Curtis High?

CHRIS. No.

FLOYD. Where'd you go? What school?

CHRIS. McKee VoTech, and I spent one year in an honors program at New Dorp. I never went to Curtis.

FLOYD. I saw you somewhere. (*Chris crosses to the bookcase endtable with Floyd tracking him.*)

16

CHRIS. I would have remembered. You know, I also think if Margaret Mead had first came to Staten Island, she wouldn't have had to spend all those years studying the abnormal behavior of Savages in Samoa.

FLOYD. It'll come back. Don't worry.

CHRIS. I'm not worried . . .

FLOYD. Could you tell me a little about that voice of yours? Is that an accent, or is your voice naturally strange and plentiful?

CHRIS. Actually, I did have a sibilant "s" and a lot of trouble with diphthongs, but they gave me speech classes so I'm not as shy about talking as I used to be. I'm really impressed by your books, Mr. DiPardi.

FLOYD. Are you *really?*

CHRIS. You have a lot of psychological literature for a shipyard worker. Very riveting.

FLOYD. I figured you'd like my books. Feel free not to use them at any time.

CHRIS. I'm very sorry about your mother, Mr. DiPardi.

FLOYD. And I'm very sorry about *your* mother.

CHRIS. She's really a very remarkable person, Mr. DiPardi. She's had to support us since my father left . . .

FLOYD. Yes, and so you two are sort of a travelling vulture team now, aren't you? You get a little dying one here, a little dying one there. Nice.

CHRIS. My mother's a very brave woman, Mr. DiPardi. You'll see how she'll be there when you and your mom really need her. She's able to do things nobody else can. (*Mrs. Boyd comes up from the hallway.*)

MRS. BOYD. (*To Chris.*) I thought I told you to get upstairs. I want to give Mr. DiPardi some privacy in his own home.

FLOYD. I do love privacy. (*Chris starts taking his suitcase and shopping bags upstairs.*)

MRS. BOYD. This is his area down here.

FLOYD. Yes, my *area* . . .

MRS. BOYD. (*To Chris.*) You've got a full view of the street and a beautiful elm tree.

FLOYD. Great squirrels.

MRS. BOYD. You'll be very comfortable up there.

17

FLOYD. Spiders the size of dinner plates.

MRS. BOYD. Mr. DiPardi, your mother's sleeping. I gave her a shot. Now, if you'll be excusing us . . .

FLOYD. I'll be excusing you . . .

MRS. BOYD. Thank you . . .

FLOYD. You just make a timetable, and we'll be snapping to, snapping to. It's going to be a regular James Ewing Hospital around here.

MRS. BOYD. (*To Floyd — indicating her suitcase.*) Then we'll get along fine. When you get a moment, would you mind puting my suitcase in the back room for me?

FLOYD. Sorry, no bellhop services.

MRS. BOYD. Oh, look, I really cannot do everything myself.

FLOYD. Well, you've got your boy and that's quite a boy. Quite a boy you've got there . . . (*Mrs. Boyd climbs the stairs into the attic room. Below, Floyd pauses, and then exits into his mother's room, carrying Mrs. Boyd's suitcase. Full lighting comes up on the attic room as Chris walks into it. Chris takes off his coat, dropping it on the mattress, and starts unpacking the things from the shopping bags, most vitally, several shoeboxes which contain his figures. He sets them carefully on a shelf.*)

MRS. BOYD. (*Entering.*) I suppose we've had worse, although it's the first time, I believe, I've been employed by a dipsomaniacal longshoreman. Hang that coat up. I do really wish you'd get rid of it. (*Chris takes a hanger out of one of the bags, puts the coat on it and suspends it from a hook on the wall. From the sheer size of it we know it doesn't belong to the boy, that more than likely it was his father's. At all times he handles the coat with great care and reverence. Mrs. Boyd sits on the bed folding the socks that Chris has tossed onto the floor from inside one of the bags.*) The money's good. We'll just make do. I'll probably be able to squeeze an extra fifty out of the undertaker.

CHRIS. Are you going to use O'Malley's or Orben's this time?

MRS. BOYD. Orben's. We'll have what we need soon, Chris. A house of our own. I won't have to drag you around to places like this! I just know it. That's all we've got to remember. We're very, very close this time. I actually think I'm going to be able to work out a deal with this Mrs. Cirbus.

18

CHRIS. I could get a paper route, and Bobby Crabb said his father got a contract to cut swamp grass around Proctor and Gamble. They're going to hire lots of kids.

MRS. BOYD. Where there's a will, there's a way. We're almost there. I'll call her back at noon and see if she'll take a low down payment. I checked for bedbugs and rat droppings.

CHRIS. I like it. It's very atmospheric.

MRS. BOYD. I have a cot downstairs. I wouldn't call it plush, but I won't have any trouble sleeping. (*Floyd goes into the bathroom.*)

CHRIS. I just hope Mrs. DiPardi doesn't die while you're out, like what happened with Mrs. Catile. (*Mrs. Boyd notices Chris heading for the staircase.*)

MRS. BOYD. Where are you going?

CHRIS. I have to use the bathroom.

MRS. BOYD. Well, there's only one bathroom, and we can't go whenever we feel like it.

CHRIS. I'll just be a second.

MRS. BOYD. (*She reaches into the shopping bag and takes out a milk bottle, handing it to Chris.*) Here, just do it in the milk bottle. I probably could call Mrs. Cirbus by eleven, but I don't want to look completely desperate.

CHRIS. Mom, I don't want to use this.

MRS. BOYD. Look, I said there's only one bathroom. And when you do use it, you go in there and lock the door. I don't want you in anybody's way. Whenever you come down, you call right to the back for me. You'll be down there for meals only. (*Chris puts the milk bottle down and resumes unpacking — he takes the hero figure out of the box and examines it.*) There's a TV in the back room with the old lady, so you can watch it when you give me a break. Do you have to unpack those things of yours? I don't like them staring at me. Why can't you just build model Messerschmidts or PT boats like other boys? (*Floyd leaves the bathroom, slamming the door. Mrs. Boyd freezes at the noise below. She puts the socks into the suitcase.*) Shh . . . he's down there. (*Floyd goes back into his bedroom and slams the door.*) He's down there, can you hear him? This will be the last place. This is it. I can feel it. (*Mrs. Boyd goes downstairs and exits via the hall as Chris pulls a dark blue velvet*

19

cloth from a shopping bag and lays it on the floor. He takes out the hero figure — himself — and sets him carefully on the cloth. Then he begins to write in a notebook. The lights go down ending the scene.)

SCENE TWO

Later that afternoon. The lights come up on Chris in the attic room. He is working on the hero / boy figure. Harold knocks.

HAROLD. (*Calling.*) Hey, Chris! It's me. Okay to come in?
CHRIS. Sure. (*Harold opens the door and comes in, carrying sheets for the bed.*)
HAROLD. I just wanted to make up the bed. Hey, what are you doing? You making a dollhouse?
CHRIS. No, I'm not making a dollhouse.
HAROLD. I didn't mean to offend you.
CHRIS. You didn't offend me.
HAROLD. There wouldn't be anything wrong if it was a dollhouse because a lot of people have dollhouses.
CHRIS. I once even met an undertaker who had a dollhouse.
HAROLD. You did?
CHRIS. Yeah, I had to go to his luxury apartment to pick up one of my mother's commissions. I didn't even know undertakers lived in luxury apartment houses. I thought they lived in their casket showrooms, or something, but right while I was in his apartment . . . I saw he had not one, but *three* dollhouses right smack in his living room, and I want to tell you these were also luxury dollhouses.
HAROLD. No kidding? You just wouldn't think an undertaker would have dollhouses . . .
CHRIS. He told me how he had built each one of them himself and how he had carved each little piece of furniture inside each of the dollhouses, and . . . when I looked closer I could see all three of them had tiny living rooms with tiny lamps and tiny kitchenette sets with tiny Mixmasters . . .
HAROLD. That's very unusual . . .
CHRIS. And in each dollhouse he had carved a little wooden

20

mother and a little wooden father, and each dollhouse had stiff little wooden children and stiff wooden little cats — I mean, his dollhouses were filled with stiffs — and each dollhouse was sealed behind glass.

HAROLD. I never even met an undertaker. (*Harold begins making the bed. Chris helps.*)

CHRIS. Well, it's very strange shaking hands with one because you never really know where their hand has been last.

HAROLD. I cleaned the place yesterday, but I had to do a wash at the laundromat. I almost choked to death up here from all the dust. It used to be Floyd's room when he was a kid, but he hasn't been in it in years. At least as long as I've known him.

CHRIS. Harold, do you mind cueing me in on why you're always doing culinary chores and working wonders with ammonia?

HAROLD. I like helping out. Floyd helped me when my father kicked me out.

CHRIS. Why'd he kick you out?

HAROLD. He wanted me to go to work, but I couldn't hold a job.

CHRIS. Couldn't you be a soda jerk or plumber's assistant?

HAROLD. I tried, but I couldn't concentrate with all that pressure. Besides, my mother wanted me out of the house, too, so she could spend all day setting the oven timer and wouldn't miss a single bus that went by. She waves to all the route #114 bus drivers. I think she puts out a lot.

CHRIS. There was a sensuous woman at the hotel like that who'd see her husband off and then sit around the lobby, but her husband finally caught her and tried to kill her by pressing a bottle of tarantulas on her neck. At least that was the rumor.

HAROLD. My father's got his own girlfriends.

CHRIS. My father has a girlfriend, too, in St. Augustine he really loves — Miss Getters — who can inhale cigarette smoke through her nostrils.

HAROLD. (*Putting the finishing touches on the bed.*) There. You ought to be able to sleep good.

CHRIS. (*Plopping down on the bed.*) Why doesn't Floyd ever come up here anymore?

21

HAROLD. He told me some bad things happened. At least, they started here. He got caught doing something.

CHRIS. What?

HAROLD. Well, sometimes when he drinks too much he just starts talking about it. He doesn't always make sense — but his mother did something really horrible to him when he was a kid.

CHRIS. What did she do?

HAROLD. I think she caught him trying to do something with a girl up here — and his mother went berserk. He was just a kid fooling around with a girl . . . When Mrs. Di-Pardi caught him she dragged him downstairs, dragged him down to the oven, she said she was going to *burn* him — screaming that he was filthy and needed to be burned. She just kept screaming that at him. Filthy! Filthy! He says she just kept screaming that . . .

CHRIS. Burn him at the oven? Are you serious?

HAROLD. That's all he tells me when he's loaded . . . and I feel sorry for him, that he's been hurt. I know he's been very hurt.

CHRIS. He seems like a nice guy. A real drinker, but nice. (*Mrs. Boyd, wearing a fancy shawl, enters from the direction of the old lady's room. She crosses to the sink and empties a glass.*)

MRS. BOYD. (*Calling.*) Chris! Chris, come down here. I want to talk to you.

CHRIS. Okay. I'm coming. Departing the turret immediately! Departing the turret! (*Chris and Harold hurry down from the attic — and Mrs. Boyd is slightly taken aback that the two of them were up in the room.*) Harold just brought me up some clean sheets and helped me make the bed. God, it's a beauty.

HAROLD. The sheets are really clean now, Mrs. Boyd. I did them with Duz and Clorox.

MRS. BOYD. That was very nice of you, Harold. Chris, I'm going to have to get down to the bank before it closes. Those bankers charge extra for every minute you're late, whether they give you a mortgage or not.

HAROLD. (*Starting out.*) I got a few more things I need to pick up from the store. Pignola nuts and a Flako pie-crust mix. (*He exits.*)

MRS. BOYD. Chris, I don't want you talking to Mr. DiPardi or that boy. They're both extraordinarily odd, you know.

CHRIS. Harold's not bad.

MRS. BOYD. Look in the brain department; I don't think he's pulling a full train, and Mr. DiPardi certainly isn't, from what I hear. I borrowed a can of condensed milk from his neighbors next door, and did I get an earful.

CHRIS. Harold's okay, mom.

MRS. BOYD. I don't care. I won't want him up in that room with you. (*She tosses off the shawl, exits into the bedroom and returns with a shopping bag. She heads straight for the cupboard and begins filling the bag with canned goods. Chris sits at the table.*) As long as I'm at the bank by three, it'll be fine. I have made up my mind, Chris. This is definitely our last live-in.

CHRIS. That'd be great.

MRS. BOYD. We will have a house, and I'll work set hours in a hospital. We will sleep in our own beds every night. I spoke with Mrs. Cirbus, and I know she wants it to all work out.

CHRIS. I hope it does . . .

MRS. BOYD. I don't care if it is in Travis with all the Polish people and their kielbasas and kerchiefs . . . My father used to always say *where there's a will there's a way*!

CHRIS. (*As Mrs. Boyd pilfers*) Hey, mom, could you lay off the "five-finger discounts" in this house?

MRS. BOYD. Honey, it's for us. For our home. He's not going to miss a few bars of soap and cans of tuna or crabmeat. (*She moves on and starts in Floyd's room now.*) We'll have our own house, but we'll need to eat. We've got a lot of good canned stuff from the other jobs. I don't want you getting TB. Oh, my — look at the lovely coins.

CHRIS. Hey, mom, I feel like calling dad. Maybe I could go down for a little visit.

MRS. BOYD. You're not calling him on that phone. The drunk's got a lock on it, and he hides the key. It's a wonder he doesn't lock up his bars of Lux and Twenty-Mule-Team Borax!

CHRIS. (*Crossing to the telephone on the end table.*) I can tap it and get the opertor. She could dial it.

MRS. BOYD. (*Returning from the bedroom.*) Operators are

rude, not stupid. She'll want to know why *you* don't dial it yourself. (*A noise from the back bedroom.*) Mrs. DiPardi keeps throwing a big wooden crucifix on the floor. And did you see the Madonna in the back yard near that cheap, above-ground swimming pool? This whole place is infested with contradictions. (*Mrs. Boyd goes out the back door to the pantry. Chris taps the connect button on the phone.*)

CHRIS. (*Into phone.*) Hello, operator. Yes, listen, I've been having some trouble reaching a number in Florida. I was wondering if you could try it for me? (*Beat.*) I'm telling you, I *did* try to dial the long distance operator! Hey! (*He hangs up, starts searching for the key.*) How'd you call Mrs. Cirbus before?

MRS. BOYD. (*Entering with more canned goods.*) Oh, *I* found the key.

CHRIS. You know where it is?

MRS. BOYD. Of course I do, but I'm not telling you. (*Mrs. DiPardi starts to moan.*) Listen to her screaming for me! She's got all those clothes and I just wanted to borrow this shawl. She kept screaming, "Take it off! Take it off!" And she refused to take her heart pills.

CHRIS. (*Searching.*) Where's the key, mom?

MRS. BOYD. (*At the cupboard under the sink.*) Forget it. What do you think, you're going to call *them* in "Ponce de Leon Land" and they're going to say *come on down?*! Your father doesn't want to see you. Oh, Chris, Mrs. Cirbus told me her movers will not be able to get her pianola out unless they rip out a window on the side room. I told her I'd buy it. You pump it with your feet and it plays things like "Isle of Capri!"

CHRIS. Momma, please stop taking things. Please!

MRS. BOYD. (*Stopping and raising her empty hands.*) Fine.

CHRIS. Is the key in one of these photo albums? At least give me a hint.

MRS. BOYD. (*Crossing up to attic room and hiding the bag behind Chris's coat.*) No, the key is not in one of those photo albums. The only key in there is possibly the key to the dementia of this hovel.

CHRIS. Harold told me Floyd's mother did something bloodcurdling to him.

MRS. BOYD. (*Returns to Chris at chair.*) Well, I spent hours going through all the DiPardi albums. Look at him with a girl at the prom. Mr. DiPardi at his high school graduation with still another girl. I went through the years . . . his fifth birthday in a play soldier's costume . . . and playing with friends . . . and his mother. One of the old albums has Mrs. DiPardi in her confirmation dress with lace, and little bows around her tiny ankles . . . his father in front of the Staten Island Maritime Commission . . . that's what it says on the building . . . And there's one album where it looks like God held the camera as he struck the DiPardis down, struck them all down. *This* album. The father with the stroke, the twisted arm and hanging jaw. His mother, you can hardly recognize her. It's like she no longer had to be attractive. And the girls disappear in this album. There is only Floyd alone, and a few shots from the service with buddies. Somewhere in this album his sobriety went kaput. But on which page? Which year? There are pictures of Mrs. DiPardi when *that* room . . . (*She indicates Floyd's room.*) . . . was hers, and *he* slept in the attic! (*She picks up albums and prepares to go.*) Oh, yes — I would like to find the key to all the mysteries in this house. Listen, the old lady's heart still sounds okay, but if she croaks tonight, I don't want you at some penny arcade.

CHRIS. Yes, mom . . .

MRS. BOYD. I never even see him touch her. I'm sure that even at the shipyard it's one drink for him and one for the compressor. He's got to have a liver as big as a goose. Chris, we're going to have a garden with lilies of the valley and Helen Traubel roses. *Oh, God, yes — where there's a will, there's a way! (She gives Chris a kiss and exits. When she is gone, he lifts the phone receiver and again taps for the operator.*)

CHRIS. Hello, operator? Yes, listen, I'm having trouble dialing long distance . . . and I was wondering if you could get it for me. (*Beat.*) No, I can't dial, operator. You don't understand — I *have no arms.* Yes, ma'am. No arms, no legs, other defects, too. (*Beat.*) Thank you, operator. Thank you very much. "Where there's a will, there's a way," operator. I always say that. (*The lights go down, ending the scene.*)

25

It is late at night. The house is dark except for Chris's room where he has added a second figure — the figure of an "Old Man" to the little stage. This represents the force that punishes the hero if he refuses to go forth on the adventure to which he is called. Chris mumbles and sounds a small gong.

Now we become aware that the TV is on in the back room. Lights up, letting the audience see through the walls. Mrs. Boyd is watching the TV with the volume turned very low. The sounds clarify to be vamping '20s music, and we see Mrs. DiPardi is cranked up in the hospital bed — she wakes up to see the TV on.

MRS. DIPARDI. Uh . . . uh . . . Hoo . . . Hoo . . . ver . . .

MRS. BOYD. (*Puzzled.*) Hoover? On the TV? You want to know if it's Hoover? Hoover what? I can't understand you, Mrs. DiPardi . . .

MRS. DIPARDI. Jay . . . Jay . . .

MRS. BOYD. No, Mrs. DiPardi, that is not J. Edgar Hoover. No, it is not. It is Stan Laurel. Yes. Stan Laurel . . . another comedian. (*Mrs. DiPardi begins to laugh.*) Yes, Laurel and Hardy. Yes. They are going to fall out a window and be hit by a piano. Yes, Mrs. DiPardi. And then hit by a train . . . (*Mrs. DiPardi laughs quite robustly for her condition. It's quite weird, yet humorous. Floyd lights a cigarette in bed, and the lights shift to his room. Harold is asleep in the bed. Floyd sits up in bed, unable to sleep. He gets up and goes out to the kitchen, carrying a book. Lights down in his bedroom. He pours himself a drink and puts the book away. Chris sounds the little gong as he continues to move the figures on the cloth. Floyd listens, then moves slowly up the attic stairs. He knocks gently on the door to the attic room.*)

CHRIS. Who is it? Is somebody there? (*He grabs a platform he's been sanding and plops down on the bed. Floyd opens the door.*) Oh. Mr. DiPardi . . . Was I making too much noise?

FLOYD. (*Coming slowly, warily into the room. He closes the door behind him, leans against it.*) What are you doing?

26

CHRIS. I was just making something.

FLOYD. Yeah. I can see that. You're making something . . . What is it?

CHRIS. I'm not sure yet, but I think it's going to be the Hormann Mansion . . . that big mansion up on Grymes Hill the beer baron built for his bride until he drove her insane and put her in a sanitarium and then gave the mansion to Our-Lady-Star-Of-The-Mountain for a convent . . .

FLOYD. I don't know what the hell you're talking about.

CHRIS. Sometimes I make scenes of our Staten Island landmarks, and once I had my picture in the paper because I had made a diorama of the Buddhist Temple on Lighthouse Hill. I was thinking that's where you might have seen me — in the newspaper.

FLOYD. Jesus Christ, why are you doing this?

CHRIS. It's the way I tell stories, Mr. DiPardi. It's sort of the way I dream.

FLOYD. I'd be careful, or they might put you away in a sanitarium.

CHRIS. Don't you ever dream, Mr. DiPardi? You must have had dreams up here when you were a boy. You must know a lot about dreams from all your books.

FLOYD. I don't read anymore. Who are the little folks?

CHRIS. This one is me. I always arrive first — at least I start first in the "zone unknown." That's what all the deep blue is . . .

FLOYD. The "zone unknown." That's nice. I usually get there after a dozen boilermakers . . .

CHRIS. I did an Egyptian one once in which I was a king supervising my pyramid tomb. I had to make a lot of other people for that one. Craftsmen to make toys for dead children, a little bakery shop, a tiny slaughter house for fresh meat — and all sorts of things to assist me in the afterlife. I even made tiny coptic jars to receive my organs during mummification in which they would remove my brain by pulling it out through my nose. They put that one on display in the front window of the Mariner's Harbor Savings Bank for three weeks.

FLOYD. Sorry I missed it . . .

27

CHRIS. You must have made things up here with balsa wood and airplane glue . . .

FLOYD. I don't dream any more.

CHRIS. Everybody dreams, Mr. DiPardi. You just forget them. Maybe you daydream, which is just as good. When you're awake — don't you play out whole scenes in your head? Don't you imagine how things will be? How they could be? They're all stories. Don't you ever listen to the voices in your brain?

FLOYD. You hear voices in your brain?

CHRIS. A lot of voices.

FLOYD. I need a drink.

CHRIS. I could let you hear my voices.

FLOYD. Really? (*Chris and Floyd sit on the floor with the figures.*)

CHRIS. If I concentrate, I can repeat what they're saying. I mean, I can tell you what this Old Man is saying in my head. (*Indicating Old Man figure.*) This Old Man says I have to follow him. And I'm telling him . . . "I don't want to go . . . I don't want to go . . ." "But I've called you," the Old Man tells me. "And if you don't come, then I will laugh when you shake with fear and perish in the whirlwind." (*As the Boy Figure.*) "I don't want to go," I say, in my own brain. (*As the Old Man's voice.*) "Then your turning away will slay you, for I will not come your way again." Don't you remember anyone warning you, Mr. DiPardi? Didn't you ever stop to listen? (*Suddenly there is a shout from Mrs. DiPardi. Lights come up on the bedroom. Mrs. Boyd tries to quiet her as the TV still flickers away.*)

MRS. DIPARDI. (*Screaming as from a nightmare.*) Floyd! Please help me, oh God! Son! Sonny!

MRS. BOYD. Now, now, now — you don't want to wake up the whole house? Are you thirsty? You want water, Mrs. DiPardi?

MRS. DIPARDI. Oh, God, Floyd! Help me, Floyd!

MRS. BOYD. You'll see him in the morning, Mrs. DiPardi. Everyone's sleeping now.

MRS. DIPARDI. Floyd! Please come! He's got his hands around my throat! Floyd, he's in here!

MRS. BOYD. Now, calm down, Mrs. DiPardi. Let me fix your pillow. Nobody has his hands on you. There's no one here . . . (*Mrs. DiPardi continues shouting and resisting Mrs. Boyd's attempts to comfort her. What spills from her lips is a chilling hallucination which reverberates throughout the house.*)

MRS. DIPARDI. (*Shouting for Floyd.*) Sonny, forgive me! I'm sorry, Sonny!

MRS. BOYD. Shhhhh! You need a shot.

MRS. DIPARDI. Son! Help me! I'm sorry!

MRS. BOYD. It'll just take a moment to get a clean syringe. I boiled the syringes. I left them in the kitchen. I'll be right back, Mrs. DiPardi . . . right back . . . (*Mrs. Boyd comes down the hall to the kitchen, heading to get a syringe from the pot, as Mrs. DiPardi yells, alone, in the room.*)

MRS. DIPARDI. Floyd! Son! I'm sorry! Jesus Christ, I'm sorry. Help me! Floyd! He's flying in the air! Son, he's flying over me, son! Floyd, he's here! He's in the room! (*Mrs. Boyd rushes back to the room and tries to give Mrs. DiPardi an injection — but the old lady won't hold still.*)

MRS. BOYD. (*Unable to control Mrs. DiPardi.*) You *are* in pain, Mrs. DiPardi. Please just hold still. (*Mrs. DiPardi strikes out with even greater force — driving Mrs. Boyd to rush from the room for help. She goes to Floyd's bedroom, knocks on the door. Calling.*) Mr. DiPardi! Mr. DiPardi! (*Chris and Floyd freeze in the bedroom, suddenly awakened from their dreamworld. Lights come up in Floyd's bedroom. Harold awakens, opens the door.*)

HAROLD. What? What's the matter?

MRS. DIPARDI. (*Screaming in her room.*) Son! Help me!

MRS. BOYD. (*Shocked to see the near-naked boy.*) I need Mr. DiPardi.

HAROLD. He's not here. What's going on?

MRS. BOYD. Where is he? (*She runs to the front door.*)

HAROLD. He was here . . . He should be here . . . What's happened?

MRS. BOYD. His car's in the driveway!

HAROLD. Hey, what's the matter? (*Mrs. Boyd rushes up the stairs to the attic. She sees Floyd in Chris's room.*)

MRS. BOYD. (*To Floyd.*) What are you doing? (*To Chris.*) What is he doing here?

29

CHRIS. Nothing, mom . . .

MRS. DIPARDI. Help me, son! I love you, son, I love you . . .

MRS. BOYD. You are *never* to be up there! Do you hear me? You are never to be up there! (*Mrs. Boyd hurries back down the stairs, with Floyd slowly following.*)

MRS. DIPARDI. Floyd! Son! Please forgive me! Help me now! Come let me see you!

MRS. BOYD. (*Ordering Floyd.*) Help me give her the shot. Hold her. Just hold her! (*They go into the bedroom.*)

MRS. DIPARDI. (*Seeing Floyd.*) Son! Oh, God, son, I've got to tell you something. Thank you, Jesus, for sending him to me. Son, come closer. Please. Please listen to me . . . please . . . my son, my boy . . . (*Indicating Mrs. Boyd.*) I don't want *her.* This is for you, for you only, Floyd . . . (*Floyd, with great effort, leans over to soothe his mother. She quiets, seems happy, comforted. Suddenly she throws her arms around him, pulls herself up to his neck and bites him. Floyd lets out a cry, pulls himself loose.*)

FLOYD. She bit me! She bit me! I'm bleeding! (*Floyd flees the room, goes into the bathroom, then into the kitchen with a cloth and alcohol. He sits at the table and pours himself a drink. Mrs. DiPardi begins to scream violently again.*)

MRS. BOYD. Help me! For Christ's sake, somebody help me! (*Harold rushes in — and helps give Mrs. DiPardi the injection.*) She's as strong as Gargantua! As strong as Gargantua, the gorilla, aren't you, Mrs. DiPardi?! So strong . . . so strong . . . and such a surprisingly little lady, aren't you, Mrs. DiPardi . . . such a lovely, little lady . . . (*Finally Mrs. DiPardi calms down to a gentle murmuring, like a baby who's drunk its full. Harold comes out of the old lady's room, looks at Floyd in the kitchen — and goes back to bed. Mrs. DiPardi starts to sweetly laugh at what she sees on television again. In the attic Chris moves his figures. The hero faces the Old Man. And Chris sounds the gong again as the lights go down, ending the scene.*)

SCENE FOUR

Evening — the next week. Chris is writing in the attic

room which looks very lived-in. The screen door opens as Harold with a shopping bag and Floyd wearing a baseball cap and carrying his jacket enter.

FLOYD. (*Going straight for a drink.*) You got the turkey set up for tonight?

HAROLD. Yeah, I sliced it. It's in the refrigerator. You don't have anything to worry about. The guys can just eat it on their own. (*Harold takes out paper plates, napkins and cups from the shopping bag and sets them on the table. Floyd puts his jacket and baseball cap in the bedroom and returns.*)

FLOYD. You don't like a good time anymore?

HAROLD. Sure I do.

FLOYD. Maybe you're embarrassed. Probably that's it. Embarrassed in front of the other boys?

HAROLD. I just want to go out. I'll be back to clean up.

FLOYD. That's very nice. You want to go to the movies *again*? How many movies have you and that snot been seeing?

HAROLD. Only two, Floyd.

FLOYD. It's getting to be real buddy-buddy. You and good ol' Chris. You got the mixers. You got ginger and tonic? (*Floyd crosses to the end table as Harold unloads trays from the refrigerator onto the kitchen table.*)

HAROLD. Yeah, I got the tonic yesterday. I already did the dips and potato salad.

FLOYD. Will you look at this, the way *she* leaves the dirty dishes, she thinks we're running a regular mess hall. (*Floyd takes the dishes he has found on the end table to sink.*)

HAROLD. She's keeping your mom nice and clean . . .

FLOYD. She just comes and eats and dirties up the place — what's this? And this? Oh, my God, she's the kind that's going to be "supreming" everything, dirtying every dish she can get her hands on.

HAROLD. I'll do it.

FLOYD. Doesn't she know about good housekeeping? She's here a few days, and she's got this place congealing.

HAROLD. I'm just going to see the movie, and then I'll be back.

FLOYD. I hear your brothers screaming from the cars. One of these nights, they're going to get a big surprise.

31

HAROLD. I thought it was the guys from Rosebank.

FLOYD. You tell them and all your friends. A really big surprise. (*Floyd glances into Mrs. DiPardi's room, seeing Mrs. Boyd's not there. Then he goes into the bathroom and spots a hair.*) And she's hairing up the bathroom. You see this, strands as long as a witch.

HAROLD. My mother hairs up sinks, too.

FLOYD. The only thing she remembered to do was leave the toilet seat up.

HAROLD. The floor's clean. I used the Spic-and-Span. (*Harold reaches for a drink.*)

FLOYD. (*Checking a cabinet.*) There's no cranberries. Hey, lay off my booze, you've been sucking up all my booze. (*Chris, listening, stands at the door.*)

HAROLD. We've got cranberries.

FLOYD. I pencil-mark the bottles, now, you know.

HAROLD. We've got three cans . . .

FLOYD. No, you don't. You got no cranberries there. No cranberries in the cabinet.

HAROLD. Sure we do. I got them last week. (*He goes out the back door to the pantry.*)

FLOYD. And, Jesus, the Lipton soup packets are disappearing at a phenomenal rate.

HAROLD. (*Returning.*) I had cranberries.

FLOYD. Sure, you *had* cranberries, but the cranberries are missing now.

HAROLD. I could run down and get some more.

FLOYD. (*Looking under the sink.*) Did you see the Brillo and the Jergen's Lotion?

HAROLD. Did you check the bathroom? (*Floyd goes into the bathroom; comes out.*)

FLOYD. And my shampoo, did you see my shampoo?

HAROLD. Maybe it's in the bedroom.

FLOYD. And my silver dollars?! (*Floyd goes into bedroom; comes out and goes back into the kitchen.*) There's quite a bit of stuff missing, you know.

HAROLD. Sometimes you forget . . .

FLOYD. It's like the great Locust of Notions has hit! If I thought it was you, I'd throw you out.

HAROLD. I didn't take anything, Floyd. (*Calling up the attic stairs.*) Hey, Chris. You almost ready?

CHRIS. (*Holding in his room.*) Yes.

HAROLD. We're still going?

CHRIS. Yeah. I'm almost ready.

HAROLD. It's a good picture. Got all good write-ups.

FLOYD. (*Starting to explode.*) Yes, I'll just bet it got the good write-ups! (*Roaring.*) Somebody's stealing my stuff! Somebody stole it!

HAROLD. No—nobody stole it.

FLOYD. Somebody stole my stuff! Just stole my stuff! (*He goes running up the attic stairs two at a time. Chris barely gets away from the door before Floyd crashes into his room. Harold is right behind him, frightened for Chris.*) Where's my stuff?

CHRIS. What stuff?

FLOYD. You know, my kitchen and bathroom gems.

HAROLD. There's some cranberries and silver dollars missing.

FLOYD. And some other stuff! Where are my silver dollars, Christopher?

CHRIS. I don't know, Mr. DiPardi.

FLOYD. You took my silver dollars!

CHRIS. I didn't take anything, Mr. DiPardi. I would never steal anything from you.

HAROLD. He didn't take anything. (*Floyd bounds suddenly to the side, grabbing Chris's suitcase, tearing it open and dumping the clothes onto the bed. Then he grabs the hanging overcoat and begins ramming his hands into its pockets.*)

CHRIS. That's my coat. Please leave it alone, please leave it alone. (*He tries to get the coat away from Floyd, but Floyd shoves him down on the bed and starts feeling the coat lining. Chris jumps up to stop him again.*)

HAROLD. (*To Floyd.*) Don't rip it, huh! Come on, Floyd, be careful, you're going to rip it.

CHRIS. There's nothing in it. Nothing. Please stop, Mr. DiPardi. (*Floyd knocks Chris down on the bed with the coat and sees the extra shopping bag. Floyd empties the bag onto the floor, out come cans of cranberry sauce, soups, soap, silver dollars go flying. Harold runs to scoop up the items.*)

33

FLOYD. (*Closing in on Chris.*) I ought to take my knuckles and bounce them off your crybaby little face.

HAROLD. Leave him alone, Floyd, leave him alone.

FLOYD. (*Shouting at Harold.*) You get the hell out of here! It's between him and me.

HAROLD. It's not his fault. Leave him alone. He didn't do anything.

FLOYD. Look, I'm not going to punch him. I said I should just take my fist and shove it right through his face there.

HAROLD. Don't hit him!

FLOYD. I said get out of here! Go down and do up the cranberries. Go! (*Harold stands still, between Chris and Floyd, embarrassed, frightened for Chris.*) I just want to talk to him.

HAROLD. It's just little stuff.

FLOYD. Yeah, well, just take all the little stuff downstairs. And don't *you* swipe it. (*Harold obeys and goes down the stairs. Floyd notices a silver dollar Harold has missed. He picks it up.*) So, are you still enjoying your little stay with us?

CHRIS. I didn't take any of your stuff, Mr. DiPardi.

FLOYD. Oh, yeah, well, Chris. I just wanted to tell you one other little quirk I've got. I don't like fruits who steal.

CHRIS. (*Hanging onto the Chesterfield coat.*) I don't steal, Mr. DiPardi.

FLOYD. You steal that coat?

CHRIS. No.

FLOYD. It's quite a coat. Looks like you lifted the wrong one at the bus station.

CHRIS. It was my father's coat, Mr. DiPardi.

FLOYD. Left it behind when he split. Is he still not taking your calls?

CHRIS. Please, Mr. Dipardi . . .

FLOYD. You wait twenty years and maybe it'll fit you. Had a little flair, your pops, didn't he? (*Reaches to touch the lapel.*)

CHRIS. Don't touch it. Please don't touch it.

FLOYD. (*Floyd grabs the coat and sparks.*) In front of the St. George Theater! Or on the ferry boat. That's it. That's where I've seen you — that puss of yours, when I do the four to midnight shift!

34

CHRIS. Please let go of my coat. You don't know me, Mr. DiPardi . . . (*He takes the coat—tries to get past Floyd.*)

FLOYD. What's the matter?

CHRIS. Nothing's the matter.

FLOYD. Where are you going?

CHRIS. Please move out of my way, Mr. DiPardi . . .

FLOYD. Look, I know you didn't take my stuff, Christopher. I mean, now that my mind's getting really lucid, I can see you've got a sense of character about you. You're quite a character.

CHRIS. You've had a little too much alcohol, Mr. DiPardi. Please let me by . . .

FLOYD. It's that mother of yours, isn't it? What kind of example can she set, just dipping her hands wherever she goes. A shoplifting practical nurse. She's probably one of the most absorbing shoplifting practical nurses we've got these days.

CHRIS. (*Trying to come back from the attack.*) She's been through a lot . . .

FLOYD. Oh, you bet she has!

CHRIS. She doesn't mean to . . .

FLOYD. No? Oh, but *you're* all right, kid. I think your heart's in the right place, but your feet don't know if they're coming or going. (*Harold goes to the attic stairs and calls up.*)

HAROLD. Hey, Chris?

CHRIS. (*Calling out, grateful for the sound of Harold's voice.*) What?

HAROLD. You ready?

CHRIS. Yeah, I'm ready.

FLOYD. Yeah, I think you are. (*Floyd steps slowly aside. His intent is threatening and sexual. Chris takes his father's coat with him as he runs down the stairs and out the door.*)

HAROLD. (*Yelling upstairs.*) We'll be back, okay? (*Harold follows Chris, bounding out the screen door. Mrs. DiPardi moans from the bedroom. Floyd stays in the attic room looking over Chris's habitation. It's only now he realizes he's trespassed into his own frightening past, and his bravura melts. The lights go down, ending the scene.*)

The lights come up with the chandelier shining above a half-devoured buffet. Fifties music, sounds of splashing and shouts from an Offstage pool party, signal there is a wild time going on in the backyard. The Offstage Voices are at a minimum Floyd, two Party Boys (attendants doubling), and the laughter of at least One Girl. The strange red glow from the pool spills into the room through the kitchen windows, as Harold and Chris enter through the front. Chris is surprised at the racket, goes to look out the window at the party while Harold starts picking up the mess of clothes, beer bottles etc.

CHRIS. (*To Harold.*) What makes Floyd have a party the week his mom comes home to die? Does he still hate her for what she did to him when he was a kid?

HAROLD. He doesn't hate her. You didn't see him drive up to James Ewing Hospital everyday for three months. He brought her candy, roses, and an electric fan. Everything. Her arms puffed up like melons because the nurses stuck the needles in wrong sometimes. He went all the time and straightened them out. Subcutaneous something.

CHRIS. (*Indicating the Offstage laughter.*) Who's the girl out there? She looks pretty.

HAROLD. Floyd just uses her with the guys. She puts out more than my mother, but she charges.

CHRIS. What do you mean? (*Chris sits at the table as Harold continues to clean up.*)

HAROLD. She always wanted money. We used to all go swimming down this creek called "Second", and even when she was ten, she'd want a quarter to show anything. (*Chris turns the chandelier light up checking the buffet for something to eat.*)

FLOYD. (*Offstage. Yelling from the pool.*) Hey, turn the dimmer back down! Hey, turn it down, in there, huh! (*Harold goes to the chandelier switch and dims it. Now shadows from the pool hit the ceiling and windows of the kitchen.*)

HAROLD. He's been losing at everything lately: mushroom pool, poker. He plays the sailors that come in down at the

36

Mayfair Bar. They always beat him. I hid a plate of fresh stuff for us. (*He goes to the refrigerator and brings out a platter. The noise outside builds.*)

CHRIS. God, I'm hungry.

HAROLD. I'm having a beer, you want one?

CHRIS. Yeah. You want me to light you a Hit Parade?

HAROLD. Yeah, thanks. (*Going to the porch door and yelling out.*) Come on, keep it quiet, huh! (*The boys jeer at him from Offstage and splash even louder. The girl's laughter is heard Offstage.*) Hey, Floyd, your mother needs to rest. Come on! (*Chris turns the chandelier light up again.*)

FLOYD. (*Offstage. From the pool.*) Turn it down! I told you to turn it down!

HAROLD. (*Turning the dimmer down.*) He wants only the red pool lights on, which is what my mother always does, too. She always wants the red lights on when she goes out to Carmen's Restaurant for paella.

FLOYD. (*Offstage.*) Hey, Harold! Bring out some wine, will ya!

HAROLD. Okay, give me a minute, will ya?

CHRIS. He thinks you're his slave. I can't see what I'm eating. One party in Annadale I went to with a girl who looked exactly like Yolanda Bet Betz — Miss America — and they didn't have a light in the kitchen, so I started eating fried broccoli until I felt something strange moving around my chin, and it turned out the broccoli was covered with ants. The girl almost fainted when I tried to kiss her and there were all these little black specks crawling on my lips. (*He turns the chandelier back up a bit.*)

FLOYD. (*Offstage.*) Hey, I'm going to come in there and knock somebody's block off.

CHRIS. Sorry! (*Chris turns the light down fast and Harold begins to hurry out with the wine and a few glasses. He's intercepted by one of the wet "party boys" who grabs the wine and glasses — then goes back on out. Chris takes a good sip of his beer. Harold sits at the table with Chris.*) You ever think about getting out of here?

HAROLD. I don't have anywhere to go.

CHRIS. Maybe you could come with me down to Florida — to my father's.

HAROLD. You going there?

CHRIS. I just have to get him on the phone. I know he'd say it was all right, if he answers.

HAROLD. How would we get there?

CHRIS. We could hitchhike.

HAROLD. Hitchhike? All the way to Florida?

CHRIS. It'd be an adventure. Didn't you ever go on an adventure?

HAROLD. Not all the way to Florida.

CHRIS. That's how your whole life should be. One adventure after another. Stanley Kusben, a friend of mine in Civics class, hitched thousands of miles and sent me postcards about turning over in a '49 Ford and seeing God in a dentist's office in Boca Raton.

HAROLD. How'd he see that?

CHRIS. He had a cavity and went to a dentist who gave him nitrous oxide gas — and he pressed this ball in his hand to get a really good dose — it controlled the flow of the gas — and when he went under he said he found himself in a labyrinth, and when he looked down one hallway, he saw God running around the corner, so he ran after God, but then God disappeared around another corner, and he ran after him again, but God disappeared around the next corner and the next and the next! And when Stanley finally came to, he said he was punching the dentist and dental assistant — and they said he had exhibited the most violent behavior they had ever seen except for one housewife who had taken gas and reexperienced the pain of childbirth. Stanley said it was the most thrilling adventure he'd ever had! (*Floyd has come in from the pool.*)

FLOYD. (*Drunk.*) Don't you think it's about time you two got in the swim?

CHRIS. I don't feel like swimming, Mr. DiPardi.

FLOYD. You must be a crackerjack swimmer, right? You probably swan-dive and jackknife and do all the Australian crawls.

CHRIS. My father used to swim to the first island off South Beach, the one with the old buildings on it.

FLOYD. What a whiz of a father you have, you lucky devil!

38

Say, did your pops have any dumbbells? Did he do any arm curls? Did your terrific pops know anything about arm curls?

HAROLD. (*Crossing to stove behind Floyd.*) You want me to make coffee, Floyd?

FLOYD. Chris, I think we've got to see your muscles so we know how much work we've gotta do. (*Chris gets up, grabs his coat and starts heading toward the stairs. Floyd follows.*)

CHRIS. I really don't want to, Mr. DiPardi, but thanks again. Good night, Harold. The movie was great.

FLOYD. What'd you see? *Bedtime for Bottle Boy!*

CHRIS. (*Freezing on stairs.*) What did you say? Excuse me — what did you say? Why did you say that?

FLOYD. I'm not the first one to ask you that, am I? I'm not the first one to find your little milk bottle, am I? I really must have a chat with Helen about your toilet training.

HAROLD. Hey, come on, Floyd, lay off.

FLOYD. Lay off? I'm not gonna lay off. *You* lay off! (*Back to Chris.*) Hey, did I say something to offend you?

CHRIS. I think you do need some coffee, Mr. DiPardi.

FLOYD. Oh, my God, now you're going to be insulting about it.

CHRIS. I'm not being insulting . . .

FLOYD. Well then, good night. You want to go to bed, go ahead. Come on, Harold, down on the floor. I want to see fifty sit-ups. I said good night, bottle boy. Your dolls are waiting for you. (*Harold crosses to chair and begins doing sit-ups. Chris confronts Floyd.*)

CHRIS. There's different kinds of sports, you know. Some kids wanted me to play semi-professional roller derby and . . .

FLOYD. Oh, I'll bet you're a great twirler. Look, I apologize. Forget everything I said. It's the booze talking. You know, it all gets into my head, like that. Forget everything I said . . . you know . . . I'm sorry . . . just go right upstairs and leak in your milk bottle.

CHRIS. My mother doesn't want me in your way.

FLOYD. (*Putting his arm around Chris.*) You in the way? Why, Chris, old boy, you're not *in the way*. You fit in as snug as a bug in a rug.

39

HAROLD. Floyd, stop . . .

FLOYD. As you may have figured out, losers like to come gobble the grub, drink the booze, puff the cigarettes! Right, Harold?

CHRIS. I'm not a loser . . .

FLOYD. Giving out my chartreuse! And, Harold, you're wearing my argyles. I asked you to please at least respect my argyles. (*Chris heads for the stairs.*) I'm not finished with you, boy.

HAROLD. I forgot about the chartreuse . . . (*Floyd gets between Chris and the stairs, driving Chris back toward the kitchen.*)

FLOYD. You see, Chris, there's a few other things I've been wanting to tell you.

HAROLD. Please, don't. Just let it go, okay, Floyd?

CHRIS. Mr. DiPardi, you don't even know me.

FLOYD. I don't know you? What do I have to know? That you don't know how to hang up your clothes when you take them off?

HAROLD. Hey, Floyd, don't . . .

FLOYD. That you don't know how to polish your shoes? Do you ever look in the mirror?

CHRIS. Mr. DiPardi, there's a few things . . .

FLOYD. Did anybody ever tell you how you walk? What you look like? How you stoop over?

CHRIS. You're king of the kids, aren't you, Mr. DiPardi?

FLOYD. Yes. And your king is talking about the potatoes beginning to grow in your ears. And your lousy hair, your gangling, pathetic dendrites! No wonder your father doesn't give a flying goddamn about you. You and your "snooky" dolls!

CHRIS. My father is proud of me . . .

FLOYD. Oh, now, Chris, we know better than that, don't we!

HAROLD. Hey, Floyd . . . (*Harold runs to protect Chris; the outside noise increases.*)

FLOYD. I'll bet you don't brush under your tongue. Your fingernails are fermenting. You slump! You take no pride in yourself! A boy's got to have pride! Jeez, you're cute when you're scared!

40

CHRIS. I'm not scared. (*Mrs. Boyd comes storming down the hall and into the room. Chris sits at the table and grabs his glass of beer.*)

MRS. BOYD. This is absolutely outrageous. Have you no consideration, Mr. DiPardi? (*To Chris.*) Chris — when did you get in? Are you drinking, Chris? What is that? What are you drinking?

HAROLD. It's my fault, Mrs. Boyd. I poured it for him, but he wasn't drinking it. (*Mrs. Boyd takes the glass and ditches it in the sink. She turns the chandelier light up.*)

FLOYD. Would you turn that back down, Mrs. Boyd? It's a little searing to my retinas, you know.

MRS. BOYD. (*Indicating the pool.*) Mr. DiPardi, if you don't stop what is going on out *there*, you're going to regret it. (*A soaking wet Party Boy comes dashing in from the backyard.*)

PARTY BOY. Hey, Floyd — you coming back out? (*The Boy dashes back out — Harold turns down the dimmer.*)

MRS. BOYD. What *is* going on around here?

FLOYD. A party, baby, a party.

MRS. BOYD. Mr. DiPardi, your mother is dying in there. Only days left, maybe not even that.

FLOYD. Well, there's not a minute to lose.

MRS. BOYD. Are you crazy? Is that what it is? You're crazy?

FLOYD. Madame, just don't shove any more of my pillow-cases and silver dollars down your girdle. Fill me up, Harold.

MRS. BOYD. I'll ignore that remark.

FLOYD. Yeah, and ignore my sundries and cranberries, while you're at it!

MRS. BOYD. Even if you despise your own mother, there are laws against exposing minors to the kinds of things you do. (*Mrs. Boyd moves toward the dimmer.*)

FLOYD. Touch that one more time, and I'm going to be very disturbed, Nurse Boyd.

HAROLD. Have coffee, Floyd . . . I'll make you instant . . .

MRS. BOYD. What do your neighbors think? How do they let you stay in this house?

FLOYD. Well, I'll tell ya. They let me stay because if they don't, I'll sell this house to Hottentots — *and they know it!* I set them straight a long time ago, and I'll set you straight now!

41

CHRIS. Mom, I think we should . . .

MRS. BOYD. (*To Chris.*) I told you to go to bed. (*Chris moves back towrd the stairs but doesn't go all the way up; he is afraid for his mother.*) Mr. DiPardi, your mother told me she came home because she wanted to die in peace.

FLOYD. And that's what I'm paying you for, kiddo.

MRS. BOYD. I think the party's over. I think if you understand what I'm talking about, the party is over!

FLOYD. (*Floyd fills his drink with leftovers on the end table.*) Hold it! The party is just starting. Did you get that, Nurse Boyd! *The party is just started!* In fact, *DiPardi* usually begins at midnight. You got that? *DiPardi begins at midnight!*

MRS. BOYD. (*To Harold.*) Can't you control him?

FLOYD. If I didn't need someone to take care of her, you'd have been thrown out the minute I saw you.

MRS. BOYD. No one throws me out, sir!

HAROLD. Floyd, you have to be up for the eight o'clock shift . . . (*Mrs. Boyd goes to the light switch.*)

FLOYD. I wouldn't touch that. That's a real no-no, Nurse Boyd. A real no-no.

MRS. BOYD. Mr. DiPardi, your mother is dehydrating. She's embalmed with morphine and those horrible experimental drugs you let them inject into her.

CHRIS. Mom . . .

MRS. BOYD. They're burning out her body! You let them biopsy her entire throat until she's got a necklace of blood. (*She moves toward the dimmer.*)

FLOYD. Don't touch the dimmer.

MRS. BOYD. I know what you are, Mr. DiPardi. (*Indicating the pool party Offstage.*) Tell them to go home.

FLOYD. (*Loudly out to the pool.*) Anybody want a beer?

HAROLD. He's drunk, Mrs. Boyd . . .

MRS. BOYD. Let me put it bluntly.

FLOYD. Do that . . .

MRS. BOYD. Mr. DiPardi, even if none of your neighbors care to involve themselves in putting an end to your illness — unless that poor lady can die in peace, I will personally see that they put you away, you slobbering, horrendous freak! (*Mrs. Boyd turns the chandelier switch on so bright it seems as if a hydrogen bomb has been detonated. Floyd smiles, then suddenly*

42

grabs a kitchen chair. Mrs. Boyd screams and runs toward the screen door as the chair arches up and crashes against the chandelier, socking it, making the pieces rain onto the room. The sounds in the pool halt. A couple of the wet Boys rush onto the back porch. Harold picks up their clothes and exits with them. Chris freezes on the stairs. Mrs. Boyd walks to the table. She and Floyd hold, staring at each other — the battle lines drawn. Lights go down ending act one.)

ACT TWO

SCENE ONE

The lights come up slowly on Chris and his little "stage."
His bed is made, almost all of the clothes have been picked
up, the coat is hanging on the hook. The main room is
spotless. The chandelier has been propped with a clothes
hanger and the vacuum cleaner is by the table. Chris has
added other "obstacle" figures to his scene. His "hero"
figure is set in opposition to the figures, and Chris speaks
in the different voices of the figures.

CHRIS. (*As Obstacle Figure #1.*) A storm, a moun-
tain . . . (*As Hero Figure.*) I still will move . . . (*As Obstacle
Figure #2.*) A cliff, and blinding thunder scream . . . a
stone, a grave . . . (*As Hero Figure.*) I still will
breathe . . . (*As Obstacle Figure #1.*) The end of
brain . . . a waiting madhouse . . . (*As Hero Figure.*) I still
will pray . . . (*Harold knocks on Chris' door — and goes in.*)
HAROLD. Good morning. (*Chris is stunned by his cheerfulness.*) Are you all right?
CHRIS. I heard you last night . . .
HAROLD. I'm sorry. He was really drunk. Do you want
some breakfast?
CHRIS. Breakfast? You're worried about breakfast? How
long have you been letting him do things like that to you?
HAROLD. I figured you knew I used to hustle. You must've
seen a lot when you were staying at the Ritz. You've seen the
boys on Stuyvesant and Hyatt . . . The boys on Hyatt
Street are cheaper than the ones on Stuyvesant, but they're a
lower class and even the cops make them do stuff. I started
out on Hyatt, but now I could be on Stuyvesant. (*Indicating
the figures.*) You don't write down your stories? You just do
them like that?
CHRIS. I write them down when they're over. (*Looks at
figures.*) I've got to get out of here. I'm going down to my
father's.

44

HAROLD. (*Sitting on the bed.*) You're really going? All the way to Florida by yourself?

CHRIS. You should come with me! You can't stay here.

HAROLD. You talked to your father? He said it was okay?

CHRIS. It'll work out. He'll come through for me.

HAROLD. How could I go? I don't have any money.

CHRIS. Tell Floyd you need to borrow some. Tell him you need an emergency visit to a chiropractor or something.

HAROLD. He can tell when I'm lying.

CHRIS. Then tell him the truth. Tell him anything. He's missing whole pieces of his mind. Anybody can see that! He gives you a few drinks and a new tooth and you think that's caring? All I know is we've got to both get out of here, or all hell is going to break loose.

HAROLD. (*Looking at the figures.*) Is that part of the story? Is that what the new "people" tell you?

CHRIS. That's part of it. That's part of what I think it's becoming.

HAROLD. Who are they?

CHRIS. They always show up — the same figures. I never even noticed about them until I had Miss Burger for English at New Dorp. She was the only one who didn't think I was a misfit, and — she was the only high school English teacher I had ever heard of who had a doctorate in Shakespearean Studies. She was so brilliant I was the only one in her class who wasn't bored and didn't throw Good and Plenty candies at her.

HAROLD. She was really very brilliant?

CHRIS. Oh, God, yes. She told me things about myself I'll never forget. The kinds of things that changed my life. Until she finally had a severe nervous breakdown and they took her away.

HAROLD. Why did she breakdown?

CHRIS. I was there! I saw it! She was reading a beautiful speech one day from *Macbeth,* and the Good & Plenty's were bouncing off her head — *boing! boing!* Until she couldn't stand it any longer — and so she opened a classroom window and leaped up on the ledge! Three stories high above a cement handball court! And she said to the class, "If you don't stop it, I'm going to jump!" And that was the first time I learned how much everybody likes action and suspense, because everyone except me yelled, "*Jump!*" But the Dean of Boys rushed in and pulled her off in time. I really miss her. She'd even let me stay after school and show her my stories. I'd perform them for her with puppets and marionettes and all sorts of things. One Saturday — she was Jewish — she let me come over to her house and turn her electricity on for her and her father — who was an Orthodox rabbi, and they gave me my first yogurt — and I performed my best stories for her. One was about a man who ran a grocery store and would mix up a ton of wheat, barley, peas, and lentils every night and then tell his stepson that if he didn't have them separated by the morning he would kill him. But I had a sorcerer appear and bring an army of ants to help him sort out the grains. And in another story I had a witch threaten to make a girl marry someone she didn't love if she didn't collect a basket of wool from a flesh-eating sheep, but an old man appears and teaches her how to gather the wool from a thicket where the monster has grazed. Miss Burger would let me tell her all my stories. She'd just sit there smiling at me, encouraging me — I even told her a story in which I invented the perfect sleeping room — a room that was painted all black with just a mattress — and a boy has fantastical dreams of heaven and death — though Miss Burger suggested I shouldn't write too many stories about God and death because she said that usually means a writer is finished — but she said she was certain I had nothing to worry about — that I was filled with life! Filled! That I had amulets! There were amulets in my stories to protect me from demons! That I'd always find a way out. I'd escape! I'd win! She was the only one to tell me I wasn't completely deranged! I was just a writer! Harold, we have to get out of here! (*Below, Floyd has come out of his bedroom. He notices the vacuum, hears the voices upstairs.*)

FLOYD. (*Calling upstairs.*) Hey, up there! Good morning, young fellas. How you doing? (*Harold hurries downstairs.*)

HAROLD. Oh, hi, Floyd.

FLOYD. (*He sees the broken glass.*) What happened? Another little accident? You break another water glass, Harold? My God, the price of glassware. You've got to be more careful.

(*Floyd gets a cup of coffee as Harold takes the vacuum cleaner out back. Mrs. Boyd enters and goes right up to Chris's room.*)

MRS. BOYD. Did you pack, Chris?

CHRIS. You didn't tell me to pack, mom.

MRS. BOYD. I'm telling you now. We're leaving. Get your stuff.

CHRIS. Right, mom.

MRS. BOYD. (*To Floyd as she returns to the bedroom.*) You're not being charged for today.

FLOYD. You're a doll, Mrs. Boyd.

MRS. BOYD. (*She returns with her suitcase, setting it by the pool table, and continues back up the stairs.*) If you'll just give me the days due me, we'll be on our way, thank you very much.

FLOYD. Oh, you're welcome very much.

MRS. BOYD. (*To Chris.*) I want to get back down to the Nurses' Registry as soon as possible. (*She goes back down the stairs where Floyd is waiting.*)

FLOYD. What are you talking about, Helen?

MRS. BOYD. You heard me.

FLOYD. You're leaving? How come?

MRS. BOYD. Give me my money, Mr. DiPardi, or I'll see you won't get another nurse near this place.

FLOYD. You're unhappy?

MRS. BOYD. Your mother has only hours to live, Mr. DiPardi.

HAROLD. Maybe it's better if Mrs. Boyd goes, Floyd.

FLOYD. You go, stupo. Take a walk.

HAROLD. Please don't call me stupo, okay? I'll get some cold cuts and creamed herring. Got a ten dollar bill?

FLOYD. No, stupo. Tens are kaput from now on. I said, beat it, stupo.

HAROLD. I said, please don't call me stupo.

FLOYD. Anything you say, stupo. (*Harold exits, and Floyd picks up Mrs. Boyd's suitcase.*) Look, let's just wait until the Grim Reaper has had his harvest, and . . .

MRS. BOYD. Mr. DiPardi, my son and I are *not* staying in this house.

FLOYD. Why not? (*Floyd puts the suitcase down and hovers around the kitchen table.*

MRS. BOYD. You're capable of great violence, Mr. DiPardi.

47

FLOYD. Look, I'll be the first one to admit to an indiscretion here, an indiscretion there.

MRS. BOYD. Give me my money.

FLOYD. Look, it's AA all the way, straight, on the wagon.

MRS. BOYD. If you call now, you just might get her back in the hospital.

FLOYD. (*Direct, emotional.*) I promised her she could die at home.

MRS. BOYD. What could a promise mean to you?

FLOYD. She begged me. She's going to wind it up at home.

MRS. BOYD. This is not a home. That boy . . .

FLOYD. *Your* boy's a bit too delicate for my taste, if that's what you're worried about. (*Chris leaves his packing and stands listening by the door to the attic room.*)

MRS. BOYD. I'm not sure you're a proper judge of what is delicate and what is not. Give me my money, Mr. DiPardi.

FLOYD. I want you to stay.

MRS. BOYD. I will call the police. I will tell them about more than your refusal to pay me.

FLOYD. Well, that's really not going to work.

MRS. BOYD. We'll see about that.

FLOYD. No, you see — two years ago, a young gentleman already blew the whistle on me. It cost me a lawyer and three thousand dollars under the table to a judge. Very little publicity, a couple of days the guys at work slipped "Floyd" — let's be euphemistic — "the deviate" notes in my locker. That's all.

MRS. BOYD. They should have locked you up.

FLOYD. Actually, my social life got better with the press. I just wanted you to know what the market price for such a trial was a few years ago. Now what is *your* price? I will pay you to stay. I will pay you more than your salary!

MRS. BOYD. What are you talking about?

FLOYD. I'm talking about a deal. I'm talking about giving you enough money, so you don't have to nickel and dime it.

MRS. BOYD. I am not interested.

FLOYD. Who are you kidding?

MRS. BOYD. I understand you are really ill.

FLOYD. And I understand you're really desperate for money.

MRS. BOYD. Some of your neighbors said they pity you —
they actually feel sorry — that you had to grow up with your
father, a man with a stroke who couldn't speak . . .

FLOYD. He wasn't speechless. The last twelve years of his
life he went, "uh . . . uh . . . uh," in a cardigan.

MRS. BOYD. Just pay me what you owe me and let me get
out of here.

FLOYD. What are you really afraid of about me?

MRS. BOYD. How can you even ask me that?

FLOYD. Look, forget the chandelier, don't worry about
your money . . . are you afraid about me and your boy?

MRS. BOYD. That's none of your business.

FLOYD. You're afraid he's going to have unusual tastes?

MRS. BOYD. No, I am not afraid of any such thing. You're
very twisted, Mr. DiPardi. I have never met anyone as abnormal as you.

FLOYD. I was married once, Mrs. Boyd. Perhaps that will
comfort you. I was married to a woman. Ironically, a woman
who was, at least physically, every bit as attractive as you are.

MRS. BOYD. Oh, I find that a bit stunning to my mind.

FLOYD. Stunning? It's not stunning. Marriage to a woman
is not a stunning achivement, Helen. Divorce from a woman
over a cheese knife — that's a stunning achievement. Now
that's something I do think I need to tell you so you can
understand . . .

MRS. BOYD. I think we'd better settle my money first, Mr.
DiPardi . . .

FLOYD. But we're *not* going to settle your money first.
We're not going to *snap* to! Let me make you understand
what I hate about you, and then you'll know how to control it
so you don't make me beat up chandeliers.

MRS. BOYD. I want my money.

FLOYD. Shut up! Can't you once shut up! You're going to
listen. You're going to listen because *then I'm going to pay you
your money, Nurse Helen!* And I'll pay you a bonus! *I'll give you
a lot of money.* (*Mrs. Boyd sits in the chair.*) You really need to
know this! My bride, Patricia . . .

MRS. BOYD. I don't want to hear about your bride . . .

FLOYD. . . . See, she and I had driven to Perth Amboy to
a department store — like Two Guys from Patterson or

something — and we needed to buy the final paraphernalia for our first dinner party — and so we headed straight for cutlery . . .

MRS. BOYD. I'm not interested in you and your bride purchasing cutlery!

FLOYD. We had to buy this cheese knife — and we were standing in front of this one department that had nice, normal ones with wooden handles — and oh, the bride's face frowned, just like your face is frowning now. You see, she thought the one I pointed to was too old-fashioned. She'd planned cheese and endive salad, and would you like a dish of Wheaties, Nurse Helen?

MRS. BOYD. You are losing your mind, Mr. DiPardi. You're on the verge of some sort of alcoholic aneurism . . .

FLOYD. And she was going to conclude with tutti-frutti ice cream topped with Kahlua — "Well, what kind of cheese knife do you want to get, sweetie?" I asked. But she wasn't too direct about it — so we looked at dozens of them. (*Chris starts down the stairs; Floyd screams at him.*) Get back up there! Get back up! Your mother and I are conversing. Don't you have *any* manners!

MRS. BOYD. Wait, Chris. Wait upstairs. (*Chris returns to the room, but sits, listening, in the open doorway.*)

FLOYD. So I kept suggesting this knife and that knife. She let me totally confess my most intimate concepts about cutlery, all of which were obviously wanting in her eyes. *And you listen to me, because this has to do with you and me, Helen!* And I told her, for Chrissake, pick out a cheese knife. I'll wait in plumbing and automotive parts. Hours later, finally, we were coming back, driving over the bridge, and she was just dying to show me the cheese knife she had decided on, but I refused to view it. And we stopped talking, so by the time our guests, Lou and Beth Kozinski, arrived at our house, we still weren't talking to each other, *and* finally — God, how I tried to avoid it — I was forced to behold the cheese knife she had selected. I had made the mistake of saying to my wife, "Patricia, may I slice you some provolone?" And she made the mistake of saying, "Yes." And I reached out and there it was, this totally remarkable silver handle and blade, hooked, curved, serrated, extruded into one single piece, an absolute marvel of incisive sculpture capable of tearing the heart out of any baby gouda, with one defect. It showed every single fingerprint. After three uses it looked so filthy I became nauseous. *On your toes, Helen!* I became nauseous with shame because I realized the saga of purchasing that cheese knife was the story of every single minute I had ever spent with any woman I had ever known. A cycle of cheerfulness to hope to deflation, to being forced to yield to a choice by some woman's smug, ultimately inept domestic fraud. *Very* much like you, Helen! Like your entrance, Helen. Like every minute of you, Helen! The whole caboodle of marital bliss flashed before my eyes in that cheese knife! And so that evening, after Lou and Beth Kozinski had left, I suggested to my bride, Patricia, that we either get an annulment or she'd better be very careful if she ever went down into a subway.

MRS. BOYD. If I understand you correctly, Mr. DiPardi, you got a divorce because of an hors d'oeuvre.

FLOYD. I just wanted you to know that when I meet your fashion of femininity, I *do* want to hurt it.

MRS. BOYD. A woman with a cheese knife . . . and a woman with a chandelier. (*Mrs. Boyd stands and heads toward the stairs.*) You want to hurt women who have strange kitchen tastes. (*Floyd stands and crosses to her.*)

FLOYD. (*Vulnerable, straight.*) Please stay, Mrs. Boyd. I apologize to you. I apologize for what I am. For everything. For what I say. For what I think. I'll back off. Keep out of your way. I don't know how to help my mother die. I can't lie about how I feel. I don't know how to change that. But I'll do anything to make it up to you. Anything. I *will* give you more money!

MRS. BOYD. My husband used to always say that — "I'll make it *up to you.*" I'm somewhat immune to that particular phrase, that fiction.

FLOYD. Do I remind you of him?

MRS. BOYD. You remind me of no one. I didn't know men quite like you existed on earth. I've only noticed more traditional aberrations.

FLOYD. Was he like me in any way? Your husband.

MRS. BOYD. He loved women, Mr. DiPardi. He loved me.

51

FLOYD. I can understand that. Would you have a small drink with me? Just an eye-opener. Just a sociable sip. (*He pours two drinks before she can refuse.*) You must have had a few wonderful years together. You must have really loved each other for a while?

MRS. BOYD. It's absolutely none of your business, but, yes, we did love each other. I know how lovely a man can be.

FLOYD. I can feel that, Helen . . . that you did love each other very much. I don't understand what could have gone wrong.

MRS. BOYD. I don't think you *could* understand . . .

FLOYD. But I'd like to try. Please just give me the chance to understand you. Did you and your husband live on the Island here?

MRS. BOYD. I don't see what difference that makes . . . although perhaps it did make a very great difference. Perhaps you'd just better give me my money . . .

FLOYD. I will. But what difference did it make?

MRS. BOYD. When my husband first passed the police exam, he worked on the Island, and he came home on time to our little stucco house on Guyon Avenue. I had a husband, and Chris had a father.

FLOYD. I hope I haven't offended you by pouring the drink?

MRS. BOYD. I'm sure you see nothing wrong with a small breakfast drink. (*Floyd offers her a chair at the table, and sits in the other chair.*) My husband and I always had a glass of wine at dinner — and he was a wonderful father to Chris. (*She sits.*) He would take him to church bazaars and South Beach, and for a Good Humor ice pop down on Hylan Boulevard . . .

FLOYD. The ice cream truck still stops there . . .

MRS. BOYD. I don't know why I'm telling you this. I don't know why I'm even talking to you.

FLOYD. Sometimes you have to talk to someone or you'd go nuts. Other times you need money very much.

MRS. BOYD. I used to try talking to my patients, but there's only so much you can share with a zombie. My husband would tell Chris the way to catch a sparrow was to sprinkle salt on the sparrow's tail. Oh, my! Little Chris running for hours after sparrows with a salt shaker in his hand! We were a family right out of the glossy sections of the newspapers. Not like on the society or celebrity pages, but we were people. And some even thought I was pretty then. Lord knows my husband was handsome in his uniform. I believed in us and our marriage. I'm boring you, aren't I, Mr. DiPardi?

FLOYD. No. I like you very much, Helen. We need to know each other . . .

MRS. BOYD. I was a wife and mother, a homemaker. I made a delicious goulash and a smoked tenderloin with sauerkraut, and I set our table with embroidered linen from my hope chest. I wasn't always what you think I am. I was a nice woman. I thought people liked me. I thought I had friends, and we'd shop for materials and patterns at Richmond Dry Goods. I felt I was loved and respected and a little important in my own way.

FLOYD. You're still a very attractive woman.

MRS. BOYD. Well, maybe once you were just as trusting and believed that life was worth living . . . and that you were a part of it. But something happened. Something was done to me. This will probably give you a big laugh.

FLOYD. I won't laugh.

MRS. BOYD. My husband was transferred to a Manhattan precinct, and so every morning he would have to leave earlier and ride the ferry across New York Harbor. And every night he would drift back. Drifting away and back, away and back, while I still clipped recipes and planted lilies of the valley, and showed picture books to my son. And then came the moment when it all changed. I think that's how all things change — in a single moment. Like death, I suppose. One moment you're alive, and the next you have death. And my husband laughed about this one moment. He laughed at our dinner table when he remembered something that had happened at work, and he wanted to share it with me. He had been in his uniform at a bar on Minetta Lane, he told me, when a young woman noticed him and said, "Excuse me, officer, but you wouldn't give a poor little girl a ticket for parking too long on a bar stool, would you?" He had so enjoyed that remark he just had to share it with me. And I think that moment when he was in that bar was the exact second my life changed for me — and I wasn't even there! I didn't know how much had changed until months later when the wife of our family doctor called, Dr. Scala's wife was on the phone telling me not to let my husband touch me because he had contracted a somewhat rampant case of syphilis. Little Chris and I had been listening to the radio, to Kate Smith and then the Longine Symphonette, and a moment later the phone had rung and Dr. Scala's wife told me not to let my husband near me until she would notify me of an "all-clear." For me, that was the moment I went crazy . . . because my best lady friends and all the glossies had told me to go crazy. They said I should go mad, and not forgive. The tradition was quite clear. Syphilis and cheating were unforgivable! So I did not forgive, and I lost my husband, my son's father, our stucco home, and then all my friends — because they were still married, and I became the desperate divorcee. And my husband — well, he drifted off permanently with the same young lady who had asked if she'd get a ticket for parking too long on a bar stool. That was just twelve, thirteen years ago. I had done what I was supposed to do. And now, the same glossies, the magazines, everyone is beginning to tell me I was wrong. Now I'm told perhaps I should have forgiven and forgotten and been supportive to my husband. I should have stood by him. Been sort of an adoring penicillin assist, I suppose. My husband still hates me. He thinks I'm the one who ruined our lives. (*She takes a sip of the drink.*) He blames me for Chris. For the dolls, the puppets, the need he has to perform and be liked. He blamed me for the fact that Chris used to imitate Carmen Miranda — the Brazilian star who did sambas with large bananas on her head — which I know is unbearably threadbare — but even I have considered that it was Carmen Miranda who single-handedly destroyed a vast section of American manhood — but I must tell you . . . that Chris used to watch me listening to Carmen Miranda, and when he saw me laughing and dancing to the records, he would look at her pictures on my albums and put on shows, and I laughed. I thought it was funny. He would wear bananas on his head, an eight-year-old boy with bananas on his head . . .

FLOYD. Helen, dear, I will give you a *two* thousand dollar

bonus if you stay two more days or until we have a cadaver, whichever comes first.

MRS. BOYD. *Two* thousand dollars?

FLOYD. *Two* grand.

MRS. BOYD. Plus my salary?

FLOYD. *Plus your salary, Helen.*

MRS. BOYD. Paid in advance.

FLOYD. Here. Here's a check. (*He goes into his bedroom and returns to the table with his checkbook.*) Here! You wait until tomorrow morning. You go the bank. Tomorrow morning you cash this, but you stay here now. (*Sincerely.*) I'll try to keep my hate under control. I will, I'll keep my hate.

MRS. BOYD. You truly do dislike *yourself*, don't you, Mr. DiPardi?

FLOYD. Perhaps I'm too self-critical.

MRS. BOYD. I was just wondering why you're using slow gin instead of a fast gun. (*She stands and crosses to call upstairs.*) We're staying, Chris! We'll be staying a little longer. (*She takes the check, picks up her suitcase and then halts.*) What a shame, Mr. DiPardi, somewhere under your rather noisy barkings, I get the feeling you could still find great happiness with the right woman.

FLOYD. So could a poodle, Helen. So could a poodle . . . (*The old lady moans offstage and Floyd stands, vulnerable.*) I can't go near her. I can't. (*Mrs. Boyd hurries down the hall. In the attic, Chris surveys his cardboard stage. He takes a fifth figure from a box. It is a monster figure. A demon. He places it onto the set as the lights go down, ending the scene.*)

SCENE TWO

In Black, the sounds of a car driving by. The lights come up on Chris dialing the phone in the living room. He is crouched behind the chair.

CHRIS. (*Into phone.*) Hello, Miss Getters? Miss Getters, this is Christopher again. Is my father there now? (*Beat.*) Oh, could you ask him to call me? Gibraltar 5-0756. Yes. (*Beat.*) Oh, good. I was just remembering the time my father and you

55

took me out for my first soft-shell crabs. (*Beat.*) And I'm very embarrassed now that I didn't know better manners when you had me to Lake Okeechobee. (*Beat.*) I said, I'm very sorry now that I didn't have better manners . . .

MRS. BOYD. (*Calling from Mrs. DiPardi's room.*) Chris!

CHRIS. I've got to hang up now. Please tell dad to call me as soon as he comes in, please. Thank you, Miss Getters, thank you. (*Chris returns the key to its hiding place and runs into the bedroom.*)

MRS. BOYD. Chris!

CHRIS. What?

MRS. BOYD. Help me lift her, that's the least you can do. Grab her before she falls on the floor. (*Mrs. Boyd and Chris carry the old lady into Floyd's room and onto his bed.*)

CHRIS. Mom, what are you doing?

MRS. BOYD. She wants to die in her own bed, and that's where she's going to die. I called a taxi. I have to go right over to Mrs. Cirbus!

CHRIS. You're putting her in his bed?

MRS. BOYD. It was *her* bed before he took it over. She's been asking to die in her own bed, and I don't think it's asking too much. (*Chris pulls her back into the hall.*)

CHRIS. Did you ask Floyd?

MRS. BOYD. I don't have to ask him very much anymore. I don't think he'd care if I kept her in the freezer, as long as he doesn't have to touch her.

CHRIS. I don't think you should . . . he really hates her . . .

MRS. BOYD. Hook up her oxygen mask. She's not going to make it through the night. (*The car squeals by again.*) I know when they're going, and this one's going. (*She returns to Mrs. DiPardi.*) This is where you belong, isn't it? Your own bed in your own house . . . (*Chris enters with an oxygen tank.*) It's only in his sick mind that she tried to burn him. She never dragged him to an oven . . .

CHRIS. Mom, he's going to go crazy. He's going to hurt someone . . .

MRS. BOYD. Don't worry about him. Just help me. Give her the full five liters. (*She leaves the bedroom, hesitates, but goes to the phone, unlocks it and dials.*)

56

MRS. BOYD. (*Into the phone.*) Hello. Hello, Mrs. Cirbus—
this is Helen Boyd. I wanted you to know I worked out the
financing, and I was just terrified that you'd sold the house
already to someone else. Your line has been busy
since . . . (*Chris crosses back into Mrs. DiPardi's room and
returns with the IV hook-up.*) Yes, I'm sure there have been
many others interested in your listing. (*Beat.*) Mrs. Cirbus, I
have a check for you. It is a second party check, but I'm
bringing it over to you now, good as gold, a very reputable
patient's family. Mrs. Cirbus, Westerleigh Savings and Loan
told me this afternoon that they will give me the loan. Oh, I
know it's Sunday. I called Mr. Lewis personally. I took care
of his father—I nursed his father 'till the end—yes, he was
my patient. He introduced the Japanese mimosa tree to
America seven decades ago—and I called him at his home.
(*Chris crosses to Mrs. DiPardi's room and returns with her crucifix and Bible. Mrs. Boyd hides the key.*) I will be there immediately . . . Of course you should finish your supper. No, I
understand. Mrs. Cirbus, I told my son about his room and
the pianola, but I did not have the chance to tell him about all
the piano rolls that came with it—the Barcarole, yes, Hu-
moresque and the Hungarian Rhapsody. You also have
twenty-seven polka rolls? (*Chris enters from hallway and sits at
the kitchen table.*) I'll tell him. He's smiling. He so wants this to
work out. He's very happy, Mrs. Cirbus. The polka is such a
spirited dance. (*Beat.*) Yes, Mrs. Cirbus, you told me about
the cockroaches. No, I've never used a Gulf Company insect
bomb. I didn't even know they made them. (*Beat.*) Please
don't sell the house before I get there. Please, Mrs. Cirbus.
We will cherish your home. We will love it and give our
hearts to it. Our hearts! Oh, thank you, Mrs. Cirbus, thank
you. (*She hangs up.*)
CHRIS. You've got to go out? (*Mrs. Boyd goes into Mrs. Di-
Pardi's room and returns with hat, gloves and pocketbook.*)
MRS. BOYD. Don't worry. I sedated her enough to keep her
on Mars until I get back.
CHRIS. I told Harold I'd meet him for a pizza.
MRS. BOYD. A pizza? We are about to get our own *house*.
Our own *house*, and you are thinking about a pizza?
CHRIS. I told him . . .

57

MRS. BOYD. Well, you'll just have to wait until I get back. I'll bring you a Chunky. I left the doctor's number in her Bible in case she does something extreme. And if it does look bad, you might slip the crucifix into her hand. Now I *know* God wants us to have this house, Chris. Oh, and she doesn't want any more of her heart pills. Even she knows keeping that heart going with those chemicals is ridiculous at this point. (*A car horn.*) That's the taxi. I'll be back. Wish us luck. (*She gives Chris a kiss and runs out . . . The sounds of a car driving away. The old lady begins to stir in her bed. She groans. Chris looks in on Mrs. DiPardi.*)

CHRIS. You okay, Mrs. DiPardi? Can I get you anything? (*She doesn't answer; just opens her mouth as though to speak, but no words come out. She closes her eyes again.*) Do you need anything? *Ich habe viele Deutsche gedichte auswendig gelearnt!* That means, I've learned many German poems by heart. I learned how to say it in German class. It's not true, but it sounds good, eh? *Ich habe viele Deutsche gedichte auswendig gelearnt.*

MRS. DIPARDI. Are you his . . . are you . . . his dolly? Please help me, dolly . . . (*The old lady starts to smile, then cough. Chris comes closer, to help her.*)

CHRIS. Are you all right? I'm not a . . . dolly . . .

MRS. DIPARDI. Help me . . . please help me . . . please . . . dolly . . .

CHRIS. The pillows. You want me to prop up your pillows?

MRS. DIPARDI. No, dolly . . . (*Chris starts carefully fixing her pillows, but the old lady's arms suddenly shoot out, grabbing for Chris. The car squeals by. Chris screams and escapes her grasp. Harold enters from the porch carrying a dress on a hanger and a beat-up suitcase. He drops his suitcase at the door and rushes to Chris who has run in from the bedroom.*)

HAROLD. What happened?

CHRIS. She tried to bite *me* this time! (*Harold goes to Mrs. DiPardi's room, then Floyd's.*)

HAROLD. What's she doing in Floyd's bed?

CHRIS. My mother put her there. Where were you? I was waiting for you.

HAROLD. Trying to borrow money at the Mayfair. Floyd caught up with me — and asked me to pick up his mother's funeral dress. (*He lays the dress across the pool table.*) A waitress at the Drop Inn hemmed and ironed it.

CHRIS. She asked if I was his dolly . . .

HAROLD. Yeah, she calls me that, too. She's always ready to drag somebody to the oven. (*Chris heads for the stairs but is stopped by Harold's voice.*) Floyd was downing boilermakers and saying he found out something about you.

CHRIS. He found out nothing about me.

HAROLD. He's drunk as hell, but says he's still checking. He kept falling off his stool.

CHRIS. Well, that really scares the hell out of me. A drunk shipyard worker's running a check on me while I'm stuck taking care of his cannibal mother! I've got to pack my stuff. (*Chris goes upstairs. Harold throws a few bottles of Floyd's liquor and some socks and underwear into a paper bag — which he sets next to his suitcase.*)

HAROLD. (*Calling up to Chris.*) Where's your mother?

CHRIS. (*Calling back.*) Out! We'll be gone before she gets back. I'll call her from the road.

HAROLD. Did you talk to your dad yet?

CHRIS. No. It'll be okay.

HAROLD. You really ought to talk to him.

CHRIS. He'll let us stay. (*Harold goes up to the attic, watches Chris put his figures back into their shoeboxes, and pack his other things.*)

HAROLD. Floyd'll never make it back until after midnight. Sometimes he just sleeps it off in a bar booth . . .

CHRIS. You didn't tell him you were leaving, did you?

HAROLD. Hell, no. I asked him to lend me a few bucks, but he said no. I could only get eight bucks out of my brother Hank. He said if I was going on some kind of trip with Floyd, he'd crack Floyd's head open. Louie stopped by, too, but he was drunk. I borrowed twenty from the bartender. You know, I wasn't going to mention it to you, but Floyd says he found out something about you and some nightwatchman in the St. George Borough Hall clock tower. He was even bad-mouthing me in front of my brothers, and they didn't like that. They said they were going to fix him. One time, Louie got some guy to hit Floyd over the head with a beer bottle. He says you know the nightwatchman in the Borough Hall clock tower — and you know Chuck somebody. (*Chris freezes for a moment.*) Chuck works nights at the Ritz where you and your mother stay between cases.

CHRIS. I don't know any Chuck.

HAROLD. He's the son of some lady electrolysist . . .

CHRIS. I don't know . . .

HAROLD. This son of the lady electrolysist says he knows you. He came in for a beer with Floyd, and I heard it myself. The nightwatchman goes into the Mayfair, too, you know . . . Is that why you want to leave, Chris, because of something with these guys?

CHRIS. No . . .

HAROLD. I was just asking, because if that's what it is, then it might be the same anywhere you go. Did you ever think of that?

CHRIS. Nothing's going to be the same.

HAROLD. (*Sitting on the bed.*) You could have told me about it. You could have trusted me. I didn't keep anything back from you. (*Chris stops packing his figures.*) Did you finish your whole story?

CHRIS. I'm not finishing this one . . .

HAROLD. Don't they tell you the end?

CHRIS. No . . .

HAROLD. Why not?

CHRIS. Because they don't.

HAROLD. They don't tell you anything?

CHRIS. I didn't say they don't tell me anything.

HAROLD. Then why don't they tell you the end?

CHRIS. BECAUSE I HAVE TO LIVE THAT PART! AND I DON'T WANT TO! I'm getting out. Are you coming or not? (*Floyd enters the house as the car squeals by. The boys stand and freeze. Floyd sees Harold's suitcase and the bag at the door, checks the cupboard. He's drunk out of his mind. He goes to the bedroom door — sees his mother in the bed. He goes up the attic stairs and finds Harold with Chris.*)

FLOYD. Oh, hi. Hello, boys. Say — you two going somewhere? Taking a few snacks and things to another movie?

HAROLD. We're going, Floyd. I'm going with Chris to stay at his dad's.

FLOYD. Oh? You're departing. Vamoosing?

HAROLD. I'm sorry. I appreciate everything. You've been a good guy, Floyd. You've been very good to me. I appreciate it.

FLOYD. You appreciate everything, eh? You really do. I can see it in your face.

HAROLD. You've been really nice. I left some chicken thighs defrosting for you in the refrigerator.

FLOYD. I have been nice to you, haven't I? It's a great comfort to know there's defrosting chicken thighs.

CHRIS. Come on, Harold . . .

FLOYD. Hey, don't you guys want a drink for the road? A little drink, and we can talk things over.

CHRIS. There's nothing to talk over.

HAROLD. Chris said they've got parrot shows and orchid stands with free orange juice right near his father's house.

FLOYD. Harold, you're staying with me.

CHRIS. He has to get out of here, Mr. DiPardi.

FLOYD. Now, Chrissie, you don't want to be rude. I'm the one that should feel insulted. I come all the way back here from a nice warm bar and find you two up here . . .

HAROLD. We have to leave, Floyd.

FLOYD. Harold, you know how much you mean to me. You've got to know that. It's only because I love you that I'm not giving you an uppercut that would knock your head off your body. (*Floyd knocks Harold down onto the bed.*) I just want the two of you to just let me talk to you. Harold, I don't want you ending up hungry next week with ringworm again, and Chris, if you want to go work the clock tower, I mean, you know, I just want to talk. A guy has a few drinks, he wants to talk, no big deal. You boys and me, see, we share a street. See, that's all that's in my mind. A nice little street! This is mainly for Chris, right? I mean, Chris, maybe you haven't quite landed in Liverpool yet, and taken the train to London, but that's what you're going to do. Have you ever been in the navy, Chris?

CHRIS. No. *You* were in the navy, Mr. DiPardi . . . (*Chris tries to leave, but Floyd forces him to sit on the suitcase.*)

FLOYD. No! See, you're going to be in your dress whites,

and you'll be in a doorway in Hamburg or Bombay—it doesn't matter where—and you'll be drinking Bacardi Rum, with a chaser of tachycardia as you remember all your books . . . (*Building with delirium.*) See, you'll be on your street, and your dolls are going to be just dolls of the evening hanging out of windows above lighted doorbells or hanging in cages . . . withered, agile ladies . . .

CHRIS. You need help, Mr. DiPardi . . .

FLOYD. I'm helping *you*! I'm helping you! (*He kneels to Chris, touches his leg.*) You see, this "boy" was unhappy with who he was . . . and so he stepped out into the moonlight and told a taxicab driver: "Take me to the whores." And he got a nice dark girl who took him to her flat, and he told her he was a virgin with the girls, but she got the "boy" going, and it was okay. But he couldn't believe he would have to make those arrangements all his life, pay in order to get the shop open, so to speak—so he dreamed there would come a sweet girl who did not have the deformed mind of a whore . . . and with this gentle, real girl he would live on the moon . . . In a dream! You know all about dreams, right Chris? This boy's dream! He and his girl would reciprocate upon the moon, caressing it until it became the whole shining ball! Full! Burning! Dance on the full moon, *kaboom*! See, Chris, you've still got that little boy's dream. (*Floyd stands, towering over Chris—reaching out to touch his face.*) I think it'd be a good idea if you just forget about it! Just forget whatever the hell goes on inside your head . . .

CHRIS. (*Standing to face Floyd.*) I'm not going to forget it, Mr. DiPardi. (*Floyd suddenly grabs him and pulls him against his body.*)

FLOYD. *You think you're going to be any different than me? You think you're going to be different than every kid that ever came through my door?*

HAROLD. Leave him alone, Floyd!

FLOYD. (*His mind snapping.*) Different than Billy who liked to hunt for deer and eat venison? Jamison, the one who joined the FBI? Leon and Teddy and the big Italian that waltzed around here in a bathrobe all the time? Or Alec? One for you, one for me, Alec. Or the Travis kid in the car? With his wet bathing suit. Or little Joey with the fifty Mexicans in

Mazatlan! Or the kid I helped pass mechanical drawing? (*Floyd is crazed, starting to drag Chris out of the room, and onto the stairs, down the stairs and toward the oven. Harold tries to calm Floyd.*)

HAROLD. Let go of him, Floyd! Let go of him!

FLOYD. (*On top of Chris on the floor.*) You filthy thing. Filthy! We just really have to burn that out of you! (*Chris escapes but Floyd catches him by the oven.*)

HAROLD. Don't . . . don't . . .

FLOYD. . . . and the fathers, thank God for the mothers and fathers warning them, the hordes, the armies, entire coast guards and high schools at my door!

CHRIS. I'm not you, Mr. DiPardi!

FLOYD. Fire! You need fire, you filthy boy! (*Floyd forces Chris onto the table, turns on the oven, opens it and starts dragging Chris to it.*) A success story of a devouring minotaur unequalled in the annals of history! And you think you're getting out? You think you're getting out? *HOW DARE YOU!*

HAROLD. (*Exploding.*) Leave him alone, you lousy, rotten bastard! (*Harold pulls Floyd off and pushes him into the pool table. Floyd collapses into the chair. Chris runs upstairs, grabs his suitcase and starts down the stairs. A taxi arrives outside — its car door slams. Mrs. Boyd enters onto the porch. She's excited as she comes through the doorway and into the kitchen. Harold closes the oven, turns it off and exits into the bedroom.*)

MRS. BOYD. (*Joyous.*) Hello! Hello, everybody! Well, hello! Something wonderful has happened! A miracle! Something of a miracle!

CHRIS. Mom . . .

MRS. BOYD. Chris, I have some news that I'm afraid is not going to wait.

CHRIS. Mom, I . . .

MRS. BOYD. (*To Floyd.*) Mr. DiPardi, now I *do* need a drink. A celebration drink!

FLOYD. Help yourself. (*She grabs a glass and pours herself a drink.*)

MRS. BOYD. Oh, Chris — everybody!

CHRIS. Mom, I've got to tell you something . . .

MRS. BOYD. It is so crazy and bizarre, but that is what I always find in this world! Mrs. Cirbus *had* another offer.

63

There *was* a completely despicable man who tried to buy out from under me.

CHRIS. Mom . . .

MRS. BOYD. And I suppose she *was* stringing me along, because he said he would pay *thousands* more than me.

CHRIS. Mama, I'm leaving.

MRS. BOYD. (*Not really hearing.*) Wait! This man showed up and tried to buy her house with a *violin!* Can you imagine! He tried to talk her into exchanging her house for a *violin!* — And she threw him out. God bless this world for lunatics! Oh, my God Chris — *we've got the house! We've got the house!* (*She runs to Chris and hugs him.*) You should have seen Mrs. Cirbus's face, the man trying to pay her with what he called a Stradivarius! and he said he was a general practitioner! (*She focuses on Chris's bag, sensing something is up.*) What's your suitcase doing down here? Your things? What is going on?

FLOYD. It's *vaya con dios.*

MRS. BOYD. (*To Chris.*) We'll stay until Mrs. DiPardi is deceased . . . We can't move in until the first . . . (*Harold re-enters with some more clothes, takes the liquor bottles out and puts the new clothes in his bag.*) What *is* going on here?

FLOYD. We're losing the boys . . . *

CHRIS. Harold's coming with me.

MRS. BOYD. What do you mean? You have a beautiful room. You'll be proud to have friends over. *Where are you going?*

CHRIS. I'm going to dad for a while. Harold needs to get away from here, too, mom. Dad'll let me stay . . .

MRS. BOYD. You're going to your father?

CHRIS. I need to live with him for a while, mama.

MRS. BOYD. Well, now that *is* something for the Mr. Ripley's "Believe It or Not" Museum. Did you tell him? Did you call him?

CHRIS. I talked to Miss Getters. Dad wasn't home . . .

MRS. BOYD. You called her, and she said she wants you, they *want* you?

FLOYD. (*Rising and crossing to hallway.*) Perhaps the two of you would like to adjourn to the attic?

CHRIS. (*Shaking and heading back up the stairs.*) I'll see you, mom.

64

FLOYD. (*Stopping him.*) Chris, I think you'd better stay and fill your mother in on some of your hobbies in the lobbies . . .

HAROLD. Floyd . . .

MRS. BOYD. What is he talking about, Chris?

FLOYD. I thought you'd enjoy knowing you and your husband's fears about Chris have been a bit conservative.

MRS. BOYD. You cannot be trusted with anything, can you, Mr. DiPardi?

FLOYD. Hey, come on, now. We're all friends. Chris just got lonely . . . you were probably doing some solo night duties, and Chris was in a clock tower where I have it, from impeccable sources, you have given a nightwatchman a number of good times! (*The sound of a car peeling rubber is heard in the distance — but closing.*)

MRS. BOYD. Chris, what is he talking about? (*The car screetches to a halt — the sound of shouting BOYS.*)

BOY #1. You drunk!

BOY #2. You lousy, filthy drunk!

BOY #1. Come on out!

FLOYD. Who the hell is that? (*Harold and Floyd run out the door.*)

HAROLD. Some guys.

FLOYD. Some guys! I know who it is. I know who the hell it is!

MRS. BOYD. (*Focused on Chris.*) Is what Mr. DiPardi saying, is what he is telling me remotely true? Look at me. Anything about it?

CHRIS. Would it make much difference if it was, mama?

MRS. BOYD. Why, yes, it would. I think it would . . .

CHRIS. I love you, mom . . .

MRS. BOYD. You love me, but you're leaving to live with your father? Now that we have a chance to live like human beings! (*Floyd enters, hovers near table.*)

CHRIS. I have to go . . .

MRS. BOYD. That is not going to happen, Chris. No, let me tell you what you have to do. You will call your father right now. Mr. DiPardi, we very much need to use your phone for long distance. I will reimburse you. (*Harold enters.*)

FLOYD. My treat. You know where the key is.

MRS. BOYD. (*Unlocking the phone.*) You will call your father. You will call him right now. It is late enough for even him to be home!

CHRIS. It doesn't matter, mom . . .

MRS. BOYD. Oh, yes, it does. *You* matter to me! *You!* Call him. Call him immediately. And you ask for time and charges. You call him now.

CHRIS. Operator, I need St. Augustine, Florida, SA-2-6118. (*She takes the phone.*)

MRS. BOYD. We want the time and charges for our call when it is finished. Yes, thank you, thank you very much. (*She shoves the phone back at Chris.*)

CHRIS. (*Into phone.*) Hello. Hi, dad? Dad, it's me, Chris. I need to see you, dad. Yes. Dad, I'm coming down to stay a while. (*Beat.*) I can't say exactly. Just a little while. A friend of mine is coming with me. Just a while. Dad, I can't talk about everything now. (*Beat.*) Yes, she's right here. Dad . . . dad, I spoke to Miss Getters, and . . . dad, I've got to see you! I've got to! Dad, please listen to me . . . please help me. Please help, dad. Dad, I don't know how else to ask you. I'm begging, dad. I'm begging. I've changed . . . I . . . dad . . . dad . . . Please, dad . . . Please . . . (*Beat.*) Okay . . . okay . . . yes, dad . . . Maybe another time. I'm sorry. I said I'm sorry. Dad . . . I miss you. Good-by. Yes, dad. (*He hangs up, bursting into tears. In a moment, the phone rings, and Mrs. Boyd grabs it.*)

MRS. BOYD. (*Into phone.*) Yes, operator. Yes, our time and charges. Thank you. (*To Chris.*) Chris, I am sorry. I am sorry for everything. (*The car of boys yelling screeches by the house.*)

BOY #1. Hit the windows! Break the windows! (*This time there is the sound of a rock hitting a windowpane somewhere in the house.*)

BOY #2. Bull's-eye! (*Harold and Floyd rush out the door.*)

FLOYD. I'll get you, you sons-of-bitches!

BOY #1. Yeah! You're getting a chain over your head!

HAROLD. Cut it out, you guys! He's calling the cops! You hear me! He's calling the cops! (*Floyd returns, followed by Harold.*)

MRS. BOYD. Some boys are a little angry with you, Mr.

DiPardi? Oh, you *are* a sucker! Somehow, if you loved them, I wouldn't even mind. You toss them a few trinkets, but you *could* have been a father to them, you could have loved them and given them something from inside of you.

FLOYD. How about a mushroom omelette? Make us some omelettes, okay, Harold? (*The old lady moans from the bedroom.*)

FLOYD. (*Ordering.*) Give her another shot, Nurse! Snap to! Snap to! (*Mrs. Boyd moves toward the old lady but then makes a decision. She exits quickly into the other bedroom. Floyd tracks her.*) Hey, now, you're not offended, are you? Hey, what's the matter? You know how rude I can be with a few drinks in me. I'm sorry, I'm really sorry. Hey, I sincerely apologize. (*Mrs. Boyd comes back with her suitcase; Chris goes in to check the old lady.*) Look, we've both had "two fingers," been a bit indiscreet.

MRS. BOYD. (*Calling to Chris.*) Come on, Chris. You can just forget this place.

FLOYD. Mrs. Boyd. I do think my mother's going to need you.

MRS. BOYD. (*To Chris.*) Chris, come with me. We're leaving! (*Chris leaves Mrs. DiPardi — comes to the living room.*)

CHRIS. Mama — I think her heart has stopped. (*Mrs. Boyd hesitates, then decides to check the old lady.*) I think she's dead. (*Beat.*) There may still be sounds. (*Suddenly, from behind the screen there is the sound of a "death rattle" from Mrs. DiPardi, and a reflective jerk of her body. It is convulsive. Horrible.*)

FLOYD. She's still alive . . .

CHRIS. No. (*Beat.*) This is how they die . . . (*Beat.*) This is after they're dead. (*Chris goes back upstairs. All of the figures are packed but the Old Man figure. He picks it up — SPEAKS to it!*) I'm finishing it. I'm going to finish it. (*Chris packs up the Old Man, puts the box in the shopping bag, takes both shopping bags, and pauses a moment to look at the coat. Mrs. Boyd does a final check of the now motionless body. Mrs. Boyd comes out to the living room and gathers her things.*)

MRS. BOYD. I've finished my part of the bargain. Come along, Chris. We're getting out of here.

CHRIS. (*Coming downstairs.*) I'm not going with you.

MRS. BOYD. You have no other place to go.

CHRIS. Leave me alone! Just leave me alone! You go, mama! Please go!

MRS. BOYD. I will not go without you!

CHRIS. (*Indicating Floyd.*) I have something to say to him!

MRS. BOYD. You will come with me!

CHRIS. I am not finished with him! I am going to talk to him! *Alone!* Get out, mama! Get out!

MRS. BOYD. I'll wait at the bus stop. If you're not out of here in minutes! Minutes! I will be back with . . . I will be back! (*Beat.*) What do you want from him, Chris? What? (*She exits.*)

HAROLD. (*To Chris.*) You're still leaving?

CHRIS. Yes. I'm going somewhere.

HAROLD. I'm not going, Chris. I'm going to stay here.

CHRIS. I know. (*To Floyd.*) You want me to call . . . to make any of the calls? . . .

FLOYD. No . . .

CHRIS. Are you okay?

FLOYD. Sure. I'm fine.

HAROLD. I'll be out back, okay, Floyd? (*Harold exits.*)

CHRIS. Mr. DiPardi — once you picked me up . . . Mr. DiPardi. About a year ago. I was hitchhiking on Richmond Terrace. I had been to the Empire Theater. You stopped in your Chevy, and I got in — your two-tone Chevy. You were drunk. You told me you owned a construction company. You said you had to stop by some offices. You took me to the brick building in front of your shipyard, and you told me to come inside with you because you had to make sure everything was locked up. You had a key for the front door. You locked the door behind us and took me into a back office. You got two bottles of beer from a small refrigerator and said we should sit down to drink them. I sat on a chair and you sat on a sofa. You leaned over the arm of the sofa. You were so drunk you had to put your beer down. You just looked at me. You didn't even talk. You held my hand. Finally, you fell asleep. I sat in the chair a long while with you holding my hand. Then I let myself out. (*Beat.*) Mr. DiPardi, I want to learn how to love . . . whoever I love . . . I

68

don't want to be ashamed and angry like you. (*Chris gathers his bags and starts to leave.*)

FLOYD. Maybe you won't . . . (*Chris halts, looks at Floyd.*) You see, I forgot to tell you why this "Boy's Dream" didn't last. Maybe it was because the *boy* was three decades old. A three-decades-old boy trying to do last minute repairs, and, by then that boy had been hurtled past the moon. M'boy . . . that part of you you don't like so much . . . don't be so afraid of it. Someday it may fit you more kindly . . .

THE END

ALTERNATE "PARTY OPENING"
FOR ACT ONE, SCENE FIVE

AUTHOR'S NOTE: In the New York Circle Rep production an "ON STAGE" party was used to open Scene 5 in Act I. Other productions may want to utilize this material in order to give more actors an opportunity to appear, however briefly, on stage. The sexuality of this scene, if used, may be subtle or as explicit as the traffic will bear.

ACT ONE

SCENE FIVE

The lights come up on a bunch of boys in various stages of undress and a young girl drinking and playing mushroom pool with Floyd. The girl is Rosemary.
There are splashing sounds from a pool offstage.
Floyd is very drunk. In the kitchen, the chandelier shines above the half-devoured buffet. A strange red glow comes from the back yard pool, spilling into the room through the kitchen windows. There is a loud cheer from one of the boys playing pool with Floyd. This boy is Joey. He is rough, more shrewd than the others.

JOEY. Right off the cushion, right off the cushion.
ROOCHIE. You're going to need more than chalk on that one.
JOEY. Did you ever swallow a cue stick? Bumper, baby. Straight ahead. Bumper, baby. (*He makes the shot, winning the game from Floyd.*)
FLOYD. (*Throwing down his cue stick.*) That's it, okay, you got it. You happy now?
JOEY. Yeah. I'm happy now.
FLOYD. Gimme another drink!
JOEY. Set 'em up.
FLOYD. The pack of you laugh until you're sick. (*Floyd exits*

*into bathroom. Chris and Harold come back from the night. They
enter with Chris still carrying his father's overcoat. Chris is, of
course, a little wary of the scene at first. Joey heads in to them from
the pool table area.)*

JOEY. Hey, Harold, how ya doing?

HAROLD. Hi, Joey.

JOEY. I was looking for you down at the Mayfair. Floyd said
you made the turkey.

LEROY. Yeah, he made the turkey, all right.

ROOCHIE. Yeah, it's some turkey. Louie and Hank are
really going to be interested.

JOEY. I don't think they knew you were making turkeys
now. Louie was hoping you'd come home. (*Floyd exits into the
bathroom.*)

HAROLD. Yeah, I've gotta stop over . . .

JOEY. Should I tell them you're going to?

HAROLD. Yeah, tell them.

JOEY. Louie doesn't like you living over here, you know.
He's starting to *really* not like it. If he gets mad enough, he'll
do something, and you know it.

HAROLD. This is Chris, Joey. Hey, everybody, this is Chris.

ROOCHIE. The nurse's kid?

CHRIS. (*Putting down the coat.*) Was my mother out here?

LEROY. Yeah, she popped out, but she popped back fast,
like a cuckoo bird. You guys going for a swim?

HAROLD. I've got to pick up the mess.

JOEY. Yeah, it's a mess, all right. Your brothers want you
out of here. Thought I'd better warn ya, before anyone gets
hurt.

HAROLD. Thanks, Joey.

ROSEMARY. Hi, I'm Rosemary.

CHRIS. Hi. (*Floyd comes out of the bathroom, goes over to Chris,
who remembers very well what happened when he last saw him in
the attic.*)

FLOYD. (*Full of drunken friendliness.*) Hiya, Chris. Good to
see you. I want to apologize about before. Never happen
again. It was just the liquor, you know, the li-
quor . . . (*Chris picks up his coat and heads back out the door.*)

FLOYD. (*Braying.*) Okay. Everybody in the pool! Come on,
everybody in the pool! We don't want "Nursie" coming out

71

again! Anything but "Nursie!" (*Floyd, and the boys stripping off the rest of their clothes, rush out.*)

ROSEMARY. I'm just watching, you hear me. Just watching. If anybody fools around, I'm leaving . . . (*She exits after them, leaving Harold and Chris alone.*)

CHRIS. Who's she?

HAROLD. Floyd uses her with the guys. She puts out more than my mother, but she charges.

CHRIS. What'd you mean? (*Chris sits at the table, while Harold cleans up.*)

HAROLD. She always wanted money. We used to go swimming down this creek called "Second," and even when she was ten, she'd want a quarter to show anything.

CHRIS. What makes Floyd have a party the week his mom comes home to die? Does he still hate her for what she did when he was a kid?

HAROLD. He doesn't hate her. You didn't see him drive up to James Ewing Hospital everyday for three months. He brought her candy, roses, and an electric fan. Everything. Her arms puffed up like melons because the nurses stuck the needles in wrong. He went all the time and straightened them out. Subcutaneous something.

FLOYD. (*Offstage. Yelling from the pool.*) Turn the dimmer down. Hey, turn it down, huh! (*Harold goes to the chandelier switch and dims it. Now shadows from the pool hit the ceiling and windows of the kitchen.*)

HAROLD. He's been losing at everything . . . CONTINUE WITH SCENE AS WRITTEN.

END OF "ALTERNATE SCENE 5 OPENING"

FURNITURE LIST

Chandelier
Rheostat – DS.L. door frame
Kitchen table
2 kitchen chairs
Stove – non practical, no light, opens UD. side
Refrigerator – light inside
Sink – running water
Bumper pool table, with balls and 2 sticks
Chair – overstuffed but small
Table – small, box-like, stores liquor and books
Mattress – for attic, on floor
Double bed – no graming, $4\frac{1}{2}' \times 6'$
Bedspread – garish
Hospital bed – period piece
Kitchen cabinets – 2 down, 6 above, practical

PROPERTY LIST

Overcoat
Call to adventure figure (Represents Chris)
3 cans of cranberries
Sheets and pillowcase
Glass
2 pool sticks
2 ashtrays
2 shot glasses
Chalk
Pall Malls with matches
2 towels
3 empty beer bottles
Suitcase (Chris)
5 pairs of socks-unfolded (Chris)
Suitcase (Boyd)
3 shopping bags
2 shirts (Chris)
Pair jeans (Chris)
Blue velvet cloth – 2'6" × 20"
6 shoe boxes
Boy figure
Old man figure
Angel figure
2 obstacle figures
Demon figure
2 hangers
8 books (Chris)
Cardboard platform (Gets cut each show)
Cardboard platform
Scissors
Blank book with pencil
Gurney
Crucifix (Mrs. DiPardi)
Rosary (Mrs. DiPardi)
Traveling IV with glucose bottle and tubing

Medical bag
Purse (Boyd)
Lipstick
Pocket mirror
Note paper with pencil
Overnight bag (Mrs. DiPardi)
Medicine
Nasal mask with tubing
Benson & Hedges
2 packages of matches
Tall glass half filled with coke
Argyle socks (Harold)
Grocery bag
Paper plates
Plastic silverware
Paper cups
Paper napkins
Pillow
Blanket
Glass of silver dollars
Wallet with tip money
Robe (Floyd)
Psychology book
Pack of Camels with matches
2 bars of Lux soap
Alcohol with washcloth
Oxygen bottle with lift
Short glass
Tippy cup
Shawl (Mrs. DiPardi)
Bible
2 beers
Plate of party food
Bottle of milk
Bowl of potato salad
Tray of turkey – fake
Half devoured turkey
Medium tray (celery, carrots, cheese squares) with small
    bowl of dip
Half devoured tray

Small bowl of dip
Coke
Tonic
Ginger ale
Wine – screw top
Dishcloth
2 bars of Ivory
Roast pan with roast – fake
Coffee pot
Pot with lid
Syringe
Rosemary
2 cans of tuna
2 cans of crabmeat
3 cans of soup
3 packages of Lipton Soup
2 wild Turkey bottles
Chartreuse
Phone with lock
Key
Books (Floyd)
5 photo Albums
Dirty dishes (bowl and glass)
Ladies wristwatch
Socks (Harold)
Underwear (Harold)
Checkbook with pen
Wheelchair
Suitcase
Dress on hanger
Paper bag
Coffee cup
3 glasses
Vacuum cleaner
3 bottles of liquor

COSTUME LIST

MRS. DIPARDI
  White nightgown
  Pink slippers
  White slip
  Two shawls
  Gray wig

MRS. BOYD
  Nurse uniform with belt
    (RN pin on collar)
  Nurse cap
  White nurse shoes
  White stockings
  Brown leather purse
  Wrist watch with leather band
  Pink floral handkerchief
  Red bathrobe
  Pale pink nightgown
  Blue bedroom shoes
  Two piece rose silk suit with scarf
  Beige heel shoes
  Beige bow shawl
  Blue sweater
  Pink hat
  Beige gloves
  Pearl necklace
  Pearl and gold earrings
  Beige stockings

ROSEMARY
  Pink pants
  Pink and yellow floral top
  Hair scarf
  Black patent leather shoes
  Red bracelet
  Hoop earrings
  Gold ankle bracelet

CHRIS
  Gray cotton pants (Calvin Klein)
  Brown belt
  Brown canvas shoes
  White socks
  White t-shirts with round collars
  Beige and brown striped shirt
  Brown with brown patterned shirt
  Blue and gray plaid shirt
  Top coat with velvet collar
  Wrist watch

FLOYD
  Maroon striped bathrobe
  White jockey shorts
  White sleeveless t-shirt
  Green and white stripe socks
  Brown leather slippers
  Blue jeans
  Brown plaid shirt
  Blue long sleeved sweatshirt
  Dodgers baseball cap
  Gray and white checked jacket
  Brown work shoes
  Blue, brown, and green plaid shirt
  Two pairs maroon argyle socks
  Wrist watch

ATTENDANT #1 / LEROY
  White pants
  White shirt with emblem
  Belt
  White loafers
  White socks with light blue stripe
  White v-neck t-shirts
  Two pairs of bikini underpants
  Two towels – beige/ducks
  Mustache

ATTENDANT #2 / JOEY
  White pants

White shirt with emblem
White low top sneakers
White socks with dark blue stripe
Belt
Plaid cap
Mustache
Black t-shirt
Blue jeans
White jockey shorts
Tattoo

ROOCHIE
Blue jeans
White jockey shorts
White sleeveless t-shirt
Beige and yellow shirt

RICHIE
Blue jeans
Orange and green print shirt
Belt
Black canvas loafers
White socks
Black framed glasses

HAROLD
White shirt with blue and black stripe
Turquoise striped shirt
Mustard brown shirt with stripes
Light blue shirt with stripe
Dark blue jacket
Blue jeans
Black Converse sneakers
Sleeveless tank t-shirts
White argyle socks
Light blue socks
Dark blue with braid socks
Maroon argyle socks

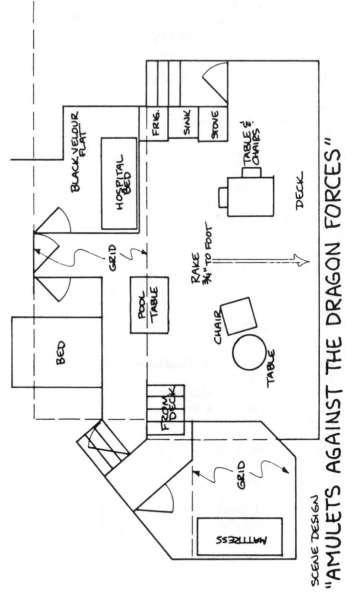

SCENE DESIGN
"AMULETS AGAINST THE DRAGON FORCES"

80

NEW
PLAYS

THE LIGHTS
by Howard Korder

THE TRIUMPH OF LOVE
by James Magruder

LATER LIFE
by A.R. Gurney

THE LOMAN FAMILY PICNIC
by Donald Margulies

A PERFECT GANESH
by Terrence McNally

SPAIN
by Romulus Linney

Write for information as to
availability
DRAMATISTS PLAY SERVICE, Inc.
440 Park Avenue South   New York, N.Y. 10016

NEW
PLAYS

LONELY PLANET
by Steven Dietz

THE AMERICA PLAY
by Suzan-Lori Parks

THE FOURTH WALL
by A.R. Gurney

JULIE JOHNSON
by Wendy Hammond

FOUR DOGS AND A BONE
by John Patrick Shanley

DESDEMONA, A PLAY ABOUT A
HANDKERCHIEF
by Paula Vogel

*Write for information as to
availability*
DRAMATISTS PLAY SERVICE, Inc.
440 Park Avenue South   New York, N.Y. 10016